ENDORSEMENTS

Go. Preach. Heal: A Practical Guide to Demonstrating Signs, Wonders, and Kingdom Power has given us a simple but profound look at what the Christian life should look like. This book is filled with revelation that is beautifully partnered with practical advice on a wide range of everyday issues that helps the reader to live the way Jesus did. This is a wonderful book.

Bill Johnson
Author, *When Heaven Invades Earth* and *Essential Guide to Healing*
Senior Pastor, Bethel Church, Redding, California
www.iBethel.org

As I read this latest work from Adam LiVecchi, once again I was challenged by his passion for Jesus. Over the past several years, I have had the opportunity to minister with Adam in a number of developing nations, both working side by side and recently as he has gone to represent me. Adam's life and ministry are marked by his zeal to preach Christ everywhere he goes. This manual overviews those aspects of the faith that are central in Adam's life. Enjoy, and let Go. Preach. Heal. provoke and inspire you.

Steve Stewart
Founder of Impact Nations
www.ImpactNations.com

And as you go, preach, saying, "The Kingdom of heaven is at hand." Heal the sick, cleanse the lepers, raise the dead, cast out demons. Freely you have received, freely give (Matthew 10:7-8 NKJV).

These are the words of Jesus to His disciples. These words are not suggestions; they are commandments. In the first chapter of the Book of Acts, after Jesus gave them these "commandments through the Spirit" about the Kingdom, He promised that they would receive power to fulfill these commandments. This promise is for us today. Why are we not seeing signs and wonders as Jesus promised? Why are we not seeing the commandments of Jesus obeyed? What is holding us back? In the following pages, Adam LiVecchi will show you step by step how to develop a Kingdom mindset, how to purpose in your heart to obey Jesus, and how to carry out the commandments of the Kingdom. The Kingdom of heaven is in you! Go, preach, and heal in the name of Jesus!

Pastor David Greco
Pastor of King's Gate Church
www.KingsGateChurch.org

Adam LiVecchi is a man on a mission to make Jesus famous to a generation that has largely strayed from a life of faith in Christ. The Go. Preach. Heal. manual will introduce believers to a gospel of faith in action, not mere words. I gladly recommend this manual for anyone wanting to mature in Christ and enter into the supernatural ministry Jesus has entrusted to the saints through the power of the Holy Spirit.

Pastor Adam Cates
Senior Pastor of the Big House Church
www.BigHouseChurch.com

Simply and yet powerfully titled Go. Preach. Heal. is a clarion call for the 21st-century church to partner with the Holy Spirit for supernatural ministry.

I'm consistently amazed how the majority of the body of Christ has ignored the Great Commission and has effectively made it the great "omission." Adam, however, offers a systematic and constructive approach as to why we must "go, preach, heal." I simply can't wait to see the impact this manual will have on believers who are hungry to be used of God!

Pastor Arthur Soto
Heaven's Gate Church
www.heavensgatechristianfellowship.com

Adam LiVecchi is a voice in the wilderness crying out for a generation thirsty for an encounter with the Living Water. He is an emerging apostolic voice seasoned in the trenches with missions and a heart for the saints. In a world inundated with quick trends and the latest fads, he grounds his book with timeless biblical truths that transcend our current trajectory. I have no doubt that this book will speak into the hearts and minds of generations yet unborn. Don't just read this. Dissect it! Wrestle with the tension of the questions he asks at the end of each chapter! May God raise up a vanguard company of visionaries who are fed up, freed up, and fired up to set this world ablaze for the kingdom of God!

Bishop D.A. Sherron
Founding Pastor, Global Fire Church
Prelate, Global Alliance
Brooklyn, New York
www.globalfirenow.com

Adam LiVecchi is a practitioner. He is a doer. His guide to *Go. Preach. Heal.* is reflective of a man who has been there and is going again. Catch his passion, catch his purpose, and join the party. He is addicted to doing what Jesus did and calling others to join him. He will not only inspire you but he will train and prepare you to follow the steps of Jesus.

Pastor Alan Hawkins
Senior Pastor of New Life City
www.NewLifeCity.org

Adam LiVecchi is a man of conviction, wisdom, and authority when it comes to the Kingdom of God. He doesn't only talk about, he lives it out day by day. He pastors, writes books, and heads up a powerful international ministry that is continually going into the nations loving the least, caring for the poor, and obeying the Great Commission. *Go. Preach. Heal.* is truly the fruit of what the Lord has taught him on this incredible supernatural journey of learning to walk in the Spirit. I truly believe that this book is an invaluable resource for new believers and mature believers alike. You will learn who you are in Christ, the great spiritual inheritance you've received, and how to practically flesh it out in your everyday life. Read through this book slowly, chew on the life-changing truths that are revealed, and put your hand to the plow, never looking back! I highly recommend *Go. Preach. Heal.* and I strongly endorse Adam LiVecchi. I believe in the man and the message. Enjoy!

Michael Lombardo
International Minister, Author of *Immersed in His Glory* and
Host of FB Live show, *Awaken Live*
www.lifepouredoutintl.org

The earth is filled with the deep cry of God's sons and daughters longing to live the life Christ died for. *Go. Preach, Heal: A Practical Guide to Supernatural Living* clearly and powerfully communicates essential truths to feed the hungry and empower the timid. Adam LiVecchi is beautifully anointed by God to cultivate leaders desiring to see Great Commission movements rather than ministry monuments. Prepare to be challenged, inspired, and transformed as you receive an impartation of the Father's heart for life, family, and ministry.

Pastor Steve Hannett
Author, *Unleashing Heaven's Breath*
Founder, EveryHouse
www.everyhousenow.org

GO. PREACH. HEAL.

GO.
PREACH.
HEAL.

A PRACTICAL GUIDE
TO DEMONSTRATING SIGNS,
WONDERS, AND KINGDOM POWER

ADAM LIVECCHI

DESTINY IMAGE® PUBLISHERS, INC.
P.O. Box 310, Shippensburg, PA 17257-0310
"Promoting Inspired Lives."

This book and all other Destiny Image and Destiny Image Fiction books are available at Christian bookstores and distributors worldwide.

Cover design by Eileen Rockwell

For more information on foreign distributors, call 717-532-3040.

Reach us on the Internet: www.destinyimage.com.

ISBN 13 TP: 978-0-7684-4542-8

ISBN 13 eBook: 978-0-7684-4543-5

ISBN 13 HC: 978-0-7684-4545-9

ISBN 13 LP: 978-0-7684-4544-2

For Worldwide Distribution, Printed in the U.S.A.

1 2 3 4 5 6 7 8 / 23 22 21 20 19

DEDICATION

I would like to dedicate this manual primarily to my spiritual parents who have given their lives to equip the church, reach the lost, and care for the poorest of the poor. Steve and Christina Stewart of Impact Nations are truly impacting the nations with the Kingdom of God. Their relentless pursuit of Jesus in the face of the least of these is challenging and encouraging. They are my heroes. Also, I am so thankful to Randy Clark who had Steve Stewart share about his water project in India at the 2007 Voice of the Apostles Conference. My life was deeply impacted from that day forward. With that being said, I would also like to dedicate this manual to Randy Clark and Bill Johnson. Your labor of truly equipping the saints for the work of the ministry is amazing; it has shaped the way a whole generation of believers thinks. We are grateful for your labor in the Kingdom.

ACKNOWLEDGMENTS

First, I want to acknowledge Jesus. You are still my very best friend. Second, I want to acknowledge my lovely wife Sarah. You are wonderful; thanks for your help. You're an amazing wife and an awesome mother. Third is my immediate family—Dad, Mom, and Aaron. Thank you so much for all of your encouraging words. I love you guys. I would also like to thank my parents-in-law for making Sarah and being so understanding of our crazy life. You have always made me feel welcome; thank you. I would also really like to thank my pastor, David Greco, because your time with me over the last few years has been priceless. I am moved closer and closer to Jesus every time I get around you. You are a blessing. My good friend Abner Suarez, you have been iron that has sharpened me and I appreciate you.

CONTENTS

WHY ANOTHER MANUAL?

Good question. It has been in my heart for the body of Christ to mature. *Go. Preach. Heal.* will help believers mature. The assignment of all believers is to turn unbelievers into believers by demonstrating who Jesus Christ truly is. Often people want to get in when the Kingdom comes. In this manual, we will look into supernatural ministry, spiritual maturity, and practical and tactical ministry that is focused on revealing Christ to the world. A changed heart leads to a renewed mind, and a renewed mind can lead to a changed world if we would only obey Jesus consistently and corporately. The man of the hour with the power is over and done with; the ministry of Jesus belongs to the saints, not to a select few. To say it another way, the one-man-show type of ministry is an old wineskin, and God will not pour new wine into it. To further drive home my point, it's *game over* for "the one man show/man of the hour with the power." This manual was written for you so that you have something tangible to encourage you as you continue the work of Jesus. The gospel has been entrusted to you; His government is on your shoulders because you are His body. You are a part of everything God is doing. Your past does not disqualify you. So put your hand to the plow and never look back.

SEVEN CORE VALUES

Core values are necessary if you don't want to compromise the truth of God's word or who He has called you to be as a person, church, or ministry. I am going to share seven core values of our ministry. Honestly, there are times I fall short of my values, so I am not perfect. However, I am forgetting those things that are behind and pressing forward with Jesus. Remember, friends, we must leave the past behind if we want to live properly in the present and be where we need to be in the future. Ministry is about knowing God and serving others. If we are going to do this effectively we must live in the present moment, not in the past or the future. You don't have to be afraid of the future or in bondage to the past. It was for freedom that Christ set you free, so stay that way and focus on the now. Focus on what the Lord is doing in your life. As we live attentively and thankfully in the now we are actually positioning ourselves for the future plans of the good that God has for us. Remember, our values speak of who we are and what we are willing to pay to follow and obey Jesus. Remember, Jesus is worth it all.

Seven Core Values of *We See Jesus Ministries*

1. To know Jesus Christ and to be known of Him. Our desire is to delight ourselves in the Lord and to be His daily delight. The first priority is to be loved by God and to love God. Sitting at the feet of Jesus is a positioning of the heart. When your heart is properly

positioned, you will have ears to hear His word and naturally your heart will burn. When your heart burns, your mouth naturally opens as God wills. We learn that lesson from the prophet Jeremiah, when he said, *"His word was in my heart like a burning fire shut up in my bones"* (Jer. 20:9 NKJV). Then you have something worth listening to that will edify your spirit as Jesus is magnified. This ministry believes that the Father's desire is to magnify Jesus in our vision and deepen our affections for Him and our devotion to Him. As this happens, we naturally represent Him accurately. As we have oil in our lamps, light naturally—or should I say supernaturally—shines in the world.

2 Long-term change comes by lifestyle change, one life at a time. Jesus taught in Matthew 5–7 and Luke 6 that He came to bring a whole new "Way" of life to the earth—His life. Jesus did not just come to give us enough truth for others to think we are not deceived. Having good doctrine or a solid statement of faith on a nice pretty website is simply not enough. To have truth and do nothing with it is a great way to build your house on sand and deceive yourself by being a hearer of the word and not a doer. This is disturbingly frequent in a society that bases too much on head knowledge and not enough on lifestyle, character, and good works that reflect biblical faith in Christ Jesus.

3 We exist to create a supernatural hunger for the Son of God in His Church so that the bride makes herself ready. As a ministry we believe that Christians can avoid problems in their lives, churches, and families by putting Jesus first. When we put Jesus first in all manners of life, we will have trials and persecutions, which are a whole lot different from problems. Jesus had no problems but a lot of persecution. So this hunger we hope to release and create and live out is so that the Church returns to her first love. We believe that hunger and thirst is the key to being filled. If we stay hungry and thirsty, we will live lives that overflow with Christ in us and give hope to a lost and dying world.

4 Jesus is the message. We preach Jesus and Him crucified. This ministry believes that Jesus Christ must be the message if change for the better is going to take place. If the message and the vessel are pure, the results will be sure.

5 We believe that God's attributes must be visible in our lives if we are really hidden in Christ. Compassion moved Jesus to feed, teach, and heal the people. Mercy from Jesus was exemplified or demonstrated when He opened four blind eyes. Grace from God looked like Simon, the Cyrenian, helping Jesus carry the cross that He would die for us on. Speaking the truth in love looked like Stephen preaching a fiery confrontational and convicting message and being willing to bleed for those who he was preaching to. Grace being released in the time of need looked like Stephen seeing Jesus standing up at the right hand of God as he was being stoned. Love has a language called *truth* and a timing called *patience* with a way of life called *long suffering*. Love is not rude even when it is right. Love looks like a slain Lamb in timeless eternity, bearing wounds that are eternal for our temporary bodies, because healing illustrates forgiveness and God is serious about reconciliation and restoration. Peace looks like rebuking a storm that threatens those whom God loves. Joy empowers us to be betrayed and forgive. Joy gives us strength to be crucified and live a happy resurrected life, even in times of suffering.

6 We value long-term relationships that are facilitated by healthy communication and a commitment to Jesus, the gospel, and one another. We believe that Christians should have long-term relationships. Our friends shouldn't change like the weather. It is more frequent to see people in the world have long-term friendships and business relationships that last a lifetime than to see Christians who have lifelong relationships and ministry partnerships. This reality is also seen in the percentage of Christians who end up divorced or live like they are divorced. It is hard to tell the world that gay marriage is evil when half of Christian marriages in the United States end up in divorce. This is a disease that the body of Christ must be vaccinated of. We desire to

make long-term relationships grow through increasing communication and strengthening commitment. Jesus is glorified as the body of Christ is unified and edified by healthy, long-lasting relationships that are centered on Christ and His purposes in the earth. (Yes, I am totally 100 percent against gay marriage.)

7 Honor is huge in the Kingdom. Lots of damage is done when things are said *about* people and not *to* people. Gossip is more natural, unfortunately, to people who have grown up in church. (That is a whole other issue for a later time.) This ministry has no interest or desire to be a part of that sort of behavior in any way. As a ministry, we believe in correction as the Bible teaches with the motivation of reconciliation at the forefront. Honor to God and His word is our first priority, and our second priority is to honor all men as the apostle Peter said. Honor is just a theory until you honor people who haven't honored you. A good friend of mine named Abner Suarez said this: "Submission is only a theory until someone tells you to be quiet and sit down." It is crucial to honor those who do not honor us. With that being said, God have mercy on me, a sinner.

These seven core values will help you form your own core values. Whether you know it or not, you have core values. Often you may hear someone say, "I would never do that" or "We must do this." What you are actually hearing is someone's core values or perhaps even their convictions. Core values define who you are and what you will do. Convictions shape who you are not and what you will not do, or even what you have done that is contrary to who you are called to be in Christ. The goal is to make disciples, not zombies. Disciples are disciplined sons and daughters, those who follow Jesus even if it costs them. The way we think and live must be shaped by God's word especially if we claim to be Spirit filled and Spirit led.

MINISTRY FOUNDATIONS

LOVE

For God so loved the world, that he gave his only begotten Son, that whosoever believeth in him should not perish, but have everlasting life. —John 3:16

The Father loved the world so much He gave Jesus. One of the simplest and purest expressions of love is giving. Jesus loved the Father so much He went to the cross and submitted to the Father's will and gave Himself that He might redeem us to God. Love has many different expressions; some of the most natural are giving and compassion. Love is patient, which means it takes time for this expression of love to be pure and mature.

True apostolic ministry isn't just about signs and wonders; it actually includes patience. Second Corinthians 12:12 states, *"Truly the signs of an apostle were wrought among you in all patience, in signs, and wonders, and mighty deeds."* In reality, mighty deeds must be compelled by love, sometimes in the context of great patience. If you ever pray, "Jesus, teach me to love people," very shortly you will be in a situation where you will either have to forgive someone or be patient with him or her. Ask me how I know. Galatians 5:22-23 states, *"But the fruit of the Spirit is love, joy, peace, longsuffering, gentleness, goodness, faith, meekness, temperance: against such there is no law."*

> **Adam LiVecchi** ✔ @adamlivecchi
> Love seeks the benefit of others at one's
> own expense.
>
> ○   ⟲   ♡   ✉

The fruit of the Spirit is first love. Love is the foundation to everything else in life and ministry. Out of love, faith, and hope, love is the greatest. Love is the more excellent way; sometimes love is the more painful way. Love seeks the benefit of others at one's own expense.

Before I speak or minster to people I often ask God to fill my heart with love for the people I am speaking to or praying for. When we understand the expressions of love it allows us to properly understand if, in fact, we are walking in love. As much as walking in love is an intentional choice to obey God outwardly, love also is an inward motivation.

> *Though I speak with the tongues of men and of angels, and have not charity, I am become as sounding brass, or a tinkling cymbal. And though I have the gift of prophecy, and understand all mysteries, and all knowledge; and though I have all faith, so that I could remove mountains, and have not charity, I am nothing. And though I bestow all my goods to feed the poor, and though I give my body to be burned, and have not charity, it profiteth me nothing* (1 Corinthians 13:1-3).

To be profitable spiritually speaking it is pertinent that we do the right thing for the right reasons. Loving God finds expression in loving people. John 15:12 says, *"This is my commandment, That ye love one another, as I have loved you."* The Greek word for *commandment* is actually "prescription." Love is just what Doctor Jesus has prescribed. Love brings healing and also prevents sickness.

Questions

1. Have you ever done the right thing with the wrong motive? If you have, ask the Holy Spirit to convict your heart. Confess what He shows you and move forward with Jesus.

   _____

   _____

   _____

2. Have you ever thought that learning patience is actually learning how to walk in love?

   _____

   _____

   _____

3. How can you love someone today?

   _____

   _____

   _____

Prayer of Impartation

Father, teach me to love like Jesus loved. Purify and sanctify every motive and ambition of mine so that all I do is motivated by love. Teach me to love You with all of my heart, mind, soul, and strength. Help me to love myself, my neighbors, my brothers and sisters, and even my enemies. Teach me the more excellent way of love, even if it hurts. It is in Jesus' name that I come to You, Father. Knowing that as You have heard Jesus, You hear me because of what He did on my behalf. Father, I just want to tell You how much I love Your Son, Jesus.

Scriptures to Meditate On

If ye love me, keep my commandments (John 14:15).

This is my commandment, That ye love one another, as I have loved you (John 15:12).

And this is his commandment, That we should believe on the name of his Son Jesus Christ, and love one another, as he gave us commandment (1 John 3:23).

TRUTH

Truth is not just a doctrine or a practice; it is a person. "*Jesus saith unto him, I am the way, the truth, and the life: no man cometh unto the Father, but by me*" (John 14:6). Truth can never be compromised in the name of "love." Love always tells the truth; love rejoices in the truth. When truth is properly applied, real freedom is experienced. When truth is wrongly applied or taken out of context, it often leads to bondage. If you know or believe the right thing and do the wrong thing, the results will be less than favorable. Truth must be applied properly for it to be true.

> **Adam LiVecchi** ✔ @adamlivecchi
> When truth is properly applied, real freedom is experienced.
>
> 🗨 ⟲ ♡ ✉

Also, just because something is true doesn't mean it is the truth. It has been said that you can be totally right, but absolutely wrong. Those who have ears to hear will hear. Great wisdom is needed when dealing with truth. Biblical truth is not to be forsaken in the name of spiritual unity. The same Spirit who brings unity is the Spirit of truth. Often the people who speak the most about truth do the least with it. Truth is a person in Christ; truth is a Spirit, hence the Spirit of truth. Truth must be spoken in love and also walked out. To speak the truth and not walk in it is to be a hypocrite.

Walking in the light or in the truth means we love people. An unfortunate reality is that truth makes enemies. *"Am I therefore become your enemy, because I tell you the truth?"* (Gal. 4:16).

Here is the good news—the enemies we make by the truth are the friends we can gain by walking in love. The love and truth connection, biblically speaking, is inseparable, so truth must transcend our culture of "political correctness." One of the things I personally find interesting is how doctrinal truth is a huge deal, but often people's lifestyle is completely overlooked. Walking in truth, using sound doctrine, and living a holy lifestyle are necessary especially if we want to be free from hypocrisy.

In a world where everything is supposedly okay, truth matters. Biblical truth is timeless and unchanging. It transcends culture and socioeconomics. All authentic ministry is rooted in truth. Our beliefs and practices must agree and line up if we are going to walk in truth. Here is a brief example. If you believe in healing, then you need to heal the sick and not just say you believe in healing. Practicing our beliefs means we are walking in truth in that particular area of life or ministry. Jesus is Lord and He desires to occupy every area of our lives, especially if we call Him Lord. Calling Jesus Lord doesn't make Him our Lord, but doing what He commanded makes His lordship a reality in our life.

Questions

1. Can you find three examples in the Bible where people spoke the truth in love?

   _____

   _____

   _____

2. If the truth will cost you, are you willing to pay?

   _____

   _____

   _____

3. Should the truth of the Bible be neglected in the name of *relationship* or *unity*? Yes or no? Please explain.

   _____

   _____

   _____

Prayer of Impartation

Father, let the Spirit of truth reveal Jesus Christ to me. Cause me to walk in truth; help me to speak the truth in love. Let the truth of Your word sanctify my heart and lead me into all truth. I ask this in Christ's holy name, that You would be glorified.

Scriptures to Meditate On

And ye shall know the truth, and the truth shall make you free (John 8:32).

But when the Comforter is come, whom I will send unto you from the Father, even the Spirit of truth, which proceedeth from the Father, he shall testify of me (John 15:26).

Sanctify them through thy truth: thy word is truth (John 17:17).

COMPASSION

Compassion moved Jesus and it should move us, especially if we say that we are "Spirit led." Real compassion leads to action. Ministry is serving one another; love should always be the motive. When love is the motive, compassion is the expression. First John 3:17 states, "*But whoso hath this world's good, and seeth his brother have need, and shutteth up his bowels of compassion from him, how dwelleth the love of God in him?*"

Adam LiVecchi ✔ @adamlivecchi
Compassion moves us in the natural and activates the supernatural power of Jesus.

Where love is, compassion is also. Wherever passion is, compassion must be also. To say we love God and not love people is just plain stupid. Compassion happens when we put ourselves in the shoes of the one who is suffering and take action against injustice. Often where great injustice is, greater compassion is needed. Compassion is what overcomes selfishness and complacency. Remember, the condition of the world shows the climate of the church. In the ministry of Jesus Christ, compassion didn't just lead to action. It led to solutions to the problems

He was addressing. For example, compassion led Jesus to solve the problem of feeding the five thousand. When He raised Lazarus from the dead He was led by His compassion. Compassion is action, not just a feeling. True compassion comes by the Holy Spirit. Compassion moves us in the natural and activates the supernatural power of Jesus.

Questions

1. Are you willing to let compassion move you?

2. How is compassion leading you today?

3. What does compassion look like when people around you may not have a serious material need?

Prayer of Impartation

Father, the same compassion that moved Jesus— let it move me. Cause me to put what I believe into action through a heart of compassion. Sanctify my compassion and give me spiritual discernment so that I am led by Your Holy Spirit as I move with You. Let compassion lead to acts of justice that cause the oppressed to go free. I ask You this in Jesus' name.

Scriptures to Meditate On

And Jesus went forth, and saw a great multitude, and was moved with compassion toward them, and he healed their sick (Matthew 14:14).

And Jesus, when he came out, saw much people, and was moved with compassion toward them, because they were as sheep not having a shepherd: and he began to teach them many things (Mark 6:34).

I have compassion on the multitude, because they have now been with me three days, and have nothing to eat: and if I send them away fasting to their own houses, they will faint by the way: for divers of them came from far (Mark 8:2-3).

POWER AND AUTHORITY

The ministry of Jesus was one of power and authority. Bill Johnson said, "A gospel without power is not good news." Jesus is our example. His ministry was one of power and authority; therefore, we need both to operate for authentic ministry to take place. There is a bit of a difference between power and authority. My pastor, David Greco, told an insightful short story about this spiritual truth: Let's say there is a power plant with a lot of power, and this one power plant gives power to almost all of New York City. In a situation where there is a power outage, only one person has the authority to turn the power back on. That man is the one who has access to the switch that gives power to the whole city. So he walks in and flicks the switch, and in a moment the whole city receives power. Authority makes power accessible.

Jesus gave power and authority to His disciples. He didn't just give it to them back then; He has given it to us as well. In the New Testament, often the word *power* is used, but it actually comes from two different Greek words. So to fully understand what He has given us, let's define these two words that are found in the New Testament.

Luke 9:1 states, "*Then he called his twelve disciples together, and gave them power and authority over all devils, and to cure diseases.*" In this verse, the word *power* comes from the Greek word *dynamis*, and *authority* is *exousia* in Greek (Strong's #G1411, G1849). However, other verses use "power" even though the Greek words are different.

Adam LiVecchi ✔ @adamlivecchi
Authority makes power accessible.

Power: *Dunamis*

As we read these two verses, we must understand that they are one story. Luke 5:17 says, "And it came to pass on a certain day, as he was teaching, that there were Pharisees and doctors of the law sitting by, which were come out of every town of Galilee, and Judaea, and Jerusalem: and the power of the Lord was present to heal them." The word translated as "power" here is *dynamis*—force, strength, and miraculous power. A few verses later, Luke 5:24 states, "But that ye may know that the Son of man hath power upon earth to forgive sins, (he said unto the sick of the palsy,) I say unto thee, Arise, and take up thy couch, and go into thine house." The word translated as "power" here isn't the same Greek word; it actually is *exousia*—authority, delegated influence, or jurisdiction. To properly understand this verse is to understand who Jesus really is. This is not just a healing; it is a sign that points to the person of Christ. His power is used to reveal His authority. We have been given both power and authority to reveal Christ to the world.

Authority: *Exousia*

And they were all amazed, insomuch that they
questioned among themselves, saying, What thing

is this? what new doctrine is this? for with authority
commandeth he even the unclean spirits, and they do
obey him (Mark 1:27).

The word for "authority" here is *exousia*—delegated influence or jurisdiction. The people in this verse weren't amazed at His power, but they were amazed at His authority. Later, the religious crowd didn't question the power of His miracles, but their question was, *"By what authority doest thou these things?"* (Mark 11:28).

Questions

1. What is the difference between authority and power?

   _____

   _____

2. Can someone have spiritual power and not be under proper authority?

   _____

   _____

   _____

3. Do healings come through power or authority or both?

   _____

   _____

   _____

Prayer of Impartation

Father, let Your power and authority flow in my life just like it did in the life of Christ Jesus. Cause me to fully submit to Your will so I can be entrusted with Your power and authority. I receive a fresh impartation of Your power and authority to fulfill all the good pleasure of Your will. Father, make me just like Jesus. It's in His name that I ask all these things, knowing He paid the price for me to receive that which I ask of You that You may be glorified.

Scriptures to Meditate On

And they were all amazed, and spoke among themselves, saying, What a word is this! for with authority and power he commandeth the unclean spirits, and they come out (Luke 4:36).

But that ye may know that the Son of man hath power upon earth to forgive sins, (he said unto the sick of the palsy) I say unto thee, Arise, and take up thy couch, and go into thine house (Luke 5:24).

Then he called his twelve disciples together, and gave them power and authority over all devils, and to cure diseases (Luke 9:1).

GOOD WORKS

What doth it profit, my brethren, though a man say he hath faith, and have not works? can faith save him? If a brother or sister be naked, and destitute of daily food, and one of you say unto them, Depart in peace, be ye warmed and filled; notwithstanding ye give them not those things which are needful to the body; what doth it profit? Even so faith, if it hath not works, is dead, being alone. Yea, a man may say, Thou hast faith, and I have works: show me thy faith without thy works, and I will show thee my faith by my works. Thou believest that there is one God; thou doest well: the devils also believe, and tremble. But wilt thou know, O vain man, that faith without works is dead? —James 2:14-20

Faith without works is dead, and dead faith can't save anyone. We are not saved by good works; however, we are saved for good works. Ephesians 2:10 says, *"For we are his workmanship, created in Christ Jesus unto good works, which God hath before ordained that we should walk in them."*

You are what God is doing! He will finish the good work he began in you. God is doing a good work in us that He might work good works through us. The Father is making us like Jesus so we reveal Christ to the world. Matthew 5:16 states, *"Let your light so shine before men,* that they may see your good works, and glorify your Father which is in heaven." Our good works make us hidden in Christ as we obey His word; this directly brings glory to the Father. The new creation was actually created for good works. Titus 2:14 states, "*Who gave himself for us, that he might redeem us from all iniquity, and purify unto himself a peculiar people, zealous of good works.*"

> **Adam LiVecchi** ✔ @adamlivecchi
> We are not saved by good works; however, we are saved for good works.

Don't let fear squash your zeal. He redeemed us from iniquity to purify us and make us peculiar in that we are zealous for good works. Being zealous to help others is the opposite of the sin nature that only cares for "self." Let me say it like this—you are not just saved *from* something, you are saved *for* something. Now is the time to step into the good works that Christ has ordained for you to walk in. Remember, walking starts with a step of faith.

Some Practical Suggestions for Good Works

1. Buy some groceries and go to a poor neighborhood. Pass out the groceries and preach the gospel to those you are giving groceries to. Heal the sick if need be.

2. Have lunch with the people in church everybody avoids.

3. The next time you go out for a meal, treat a stranger to dinner and tell them you paid for their dinner because Jesus paid for your sins and theirs. Share the love of God in a practical way.

4. Donate online to a ministry that works with "the least of these."

5. I am going to stretch you on the last two. Buy a gift card to a baby store and go to an abortion clinic and offer a gift to an expecting mother to convince her not to abort her child.

6. Go on an international missions trip.

I recommend going on a missions trip with any one of these ministries:

Impact Nations: www.ImpactNations.com

Shores of Grace: www.ShoresofGrace.com

Global Awakening: www.GlobalAwakening.com

We See Jesus Ministries: www.WeSeeJesusministries.com

HELL

Some people want to scare the hell out of you. However, God wants to love the hell out of you. It is God's desire that none should perish—that needs to become our desire. Some preachers are afraid to mention hell, not wanting to offend people. Other preachers don't like to mention it all that much because "hell preaching" has been used to manipulate people in the church world. In reality hell is real, it's hot, and it's eternal. It is where the "*worm dieth not, and the fire is not quenched,*" according to Mark 9:43-48. This "seeker insensitive" verse is repeated three times, but it is totally omitted two out of those three times in the New International Version of the Bible—but that is another message for another day. If Jesus repeated Himself three times in a row about hell, it must be pretty serious. What I find interesting is when He mentioned hell it was always to religious people. He never mentioned hell to the publicans or the woman caught in adultery or even the centurion. It's unfortunate when the body of Christ doesn't respond to heretics or manipulators properly.

Adam LiVecchi ✔ @adamlivecchi
Hell is real, it's hot, and it's eternal.

We shouldn't avoid talking about hell because people have beat the subject up or used it the wrong way to try to control people because of their own fears or insecurities. Everyone who does not accept Jesus will burn there forever, and God will not send any apology letters. There is no mail in hell. I am not writing this to be harsh. I am not angry or hurt, and honestly the church hasn't burned me all that bad either. I have chosen to include hell as a core value because Jesus valued mankind so much He tasted death for everyone so that no man or woman has to go there. If people end up there it is simply not God's fault because He gave Jesus. It's their fault for rejecting Him. Hell is real and you don't belong there, so believe on and obey Jesus Christ the Son of God.

Questions

1. Do you believe hell is a real place?

_____

_____

_____

2. Do you want people to go there?

_____

_____

_____

3. Are you afraid to warn people about hell?

_____

_____

_____

Prayer of Impartation

Father, You love the world so much that You gave Your only begotten Son. You are not willing that any should perish. Jesus, You tasted death for every man. Father, form Jesus in me until I come to the place where I am not willing that any should perish. Holy Spirit, help me to hear Your voice as I minister to the lost. Jesus, help me to bring You the reward of Your suffering. Let no one burn in hell because of my silence or complacency.

Scriptures to Meditate On

I tell you, Nay: but, except ye repent, ye shall all likewise perish (Luke 13:3,5).

For the preaching of the cross is to them that perish foolishness; but unto us which are saved it is the power of God (1 Corinthians 1:18).

The Lord is not slack concerning his promise, as some men count slackness; but is longsuffering to us-ward, not willing that any should perish, but that all should come to repentance (2 Peter 3:9).

GO

When Jesus told us to go into all the world and preach the gospel, it was a commandment not a suggestion. This is a commandment that needs to be taken very seriously. It is both our privilege and responsibility to go and to preach. The message is Jesus and His Kingdom; we will get into that later. Jesus' entire earthly stay was a mission trip. He came to seek and to save that which is lost. The church by and large is operating with an old wineskin when it comes to "going into all the world." Often in church you will hear prayers like this: "Oh Lord, bring in the harvest," or "Father, let the lost come home," etc. If we want the lost to come home, we must go and get them.

Adam LiVecchi ✔ @adamlivecchi
When Jesus told us to go into all the world and preach the gospel, it was a commandment not a suggestion.

If you are from a "prophetic church" you may hear prophecy like this: "The Lord is going to bring in the harvest" or "God is going to send us the lost." This all sounds great, except it is in direct opposition to what

Jesus commanded. Now do you see the conflict of interests? When we are operating with an old wineskin asking for new wine we are actually positioning ourselves for disappointment. If we don't guard our hearts, disappointment can easily grow into discouragement and discouragement can become disillusionment. We don't need to be discouraged because we need courage to obey Jesus and go where He has commanded us to go. Furthermore, we don't need to be disillusioned because when someone becomes disillusioned all they can see is their circumstances. When someone is disillusioned they have no real, clear vision of the future. This is obviously detrimental to the advancement of the Gospel.

When Jesus sent His disciples out to preach the Kingdom, heal the sick, and cast out devils, they returned with joy. When people come into the Kingdom (or repent of their sins) the angels rejoice. Heaven rejoices a lot more over a sinner who repents than a three-hour church service. We need our minds to be renewed when it comes to going into all the world. Stop waiting for the world to come to you and be like Christ and go to the world. I think it is quite arrogant of us when we expect the world to come to us, especially when Jesus came down from heaven to seek and save us. We need to humble ourselves and obey Jesus and go to those who don't yet know Him.

This is a serious matter; other people's salvation is attached to our obedience—no pressure though. Jesus is our example; He was sent by the Father and commanded us to go, and therefore we must. Let's listen to King Solomon describe the mission's movement. Proverbs 25:25 states, "As cold waters to a thirsty soul, so is good news from a far country." The gospel is good news and being sent into all the world includes far countries. Right before Jesus ascended to the right hand of the Father He said this to His disciples:

> But ye shall receive power, after that the Holy Ghost is come upon you: and ye shall be witnesses unto me both in Jerusalem, and in all Judaea, and in Samaria, and unto the uttermost part of the earth (Acts 1:8).

The question is not *are you called*. The question is *are you a disciple and will you obey Jesus?* (At the back of the manual I am going to share some ministries to get you jumpstarted with obeying Jesus.) John 15:16 says:

> *Ye have not chosen me, but I have chosen you, and*
> *ordained you, that ye should go and bring forth fruit,*
> *and that your fruit should remain: that whatsoever ye*
> *shall ask of the Father in my name, he may give it you.*

You are chosen and ordained. Therefore, you are called to bring forth fruit; however, if you want to bring forth fruit you must go somewhere. Bringing forth fruit is in the context of prayer. Heidi Baker says it this way: "All fruitfulness flows from intimacy." However, true intimacy always leads to fruitfulness. Fruitfulness is people coming into the Kingdom and staying there—hence, fruit that remains.

GO. PREACH. HEAL.

Questions

1. Will you go where God sends you?

   _____

   _____

   _____

2. Where is God sending you?

   _____

   _____

   _____

3. When will you go and how long will you stay?

   _____

   _____

   _____

Prayer of Impartation

Father, in Jesus' name, I pray that the Lord of the harvest would send forth laborers. May I be gripped by Your sacrifice on Calvary and follow You wherever You may lead. Give me the courage to go and wisdom as to when and for how long. Let me be fruitful in every good work and increase in the knowledge of God as I go. Bless me in my coming and in my going. It's in Jesus' name and for His honor and glory that we pray.

Scriptures to Meditate On

As cold waters to a thirsty soul, so is good news from a far country (Proverbs 25:25).

But ye shall receive power, after that the Holy Ghost is come upon you: and ye shall be witnesses unto me both in Jerusalem, and in all Judaea, and in Samaria, and unto the uttermost part of the earth (Acts 1:8).

Ye have not chosen me, but I have chosen you, and ordained you, that ye should go and bring forth fruit, and that your fruit should remain: that whatsoever ye shall ask of the Father in my name, he may give it you (John 15:16).

PREACH

Let us start where we begin and end—with Jesus. He is our example. He is the gospel. He is the message, and we are called to be His disciples; therefore, we must do as He did. His ministry was made up of three things, and we are called to do all three of those things. They are as follows: preach, teach, and heal. Matthew 4:23 states, *"And Jesus went about all Galilee, teaching in their synagogues, and preaching the gospel of the kingdom, and healing all manner of sickness and all manner of disease among the people."*

Preaching doesn't necessarily mean you need a microphone. Teaching doesn't have to take place in a church or classroom, and healing can occur wherever the sick are. At this point we need to grow up and stop making excuses about what we are not called to do and start doing what Jesus commanded us to do. Jesus said, *"Without Me you can do nothing"* (John 15:5 NKJV). Some people spend their whole time on this earth learning that. However the body needs to mature into the understanding that, *"I can do all things through Christ who strengthens me"* (Phil. 4:13 NKJV).

Preaching the gospel is not about yelling at people with a microphone. Jesus and the apostles never even had a microphone. Preaching isn't about shouting and spitting. Preaching has nothing to do with the volume of your voice. Preaching is *boldly declaring a message*. At times it may be loud, but often it's not. Confidence in our message is preaching. Meaning, we are not asking questions. We are making statements with no apologies for the message.

Preaching is easier and more effective when we know the Person we are speaking about and when we speak with confidence and authority. It's pretty rough preaching about someone we don't really know. The more we know Jesus the more confident we are in the message. Confidence must be rooted in love and humility with genuine concern for those whom we are preaching to. If it's not, the world will see right through a religious agenda. Love and compassion cause people to drop their guard and let others into their world. Love means we speak the truth with the right motives. Love is not self-seeking, meaning love does the right thing for the right reasons. Religion often does the right thing but for the wrong reasons. Our religion and tradition is actually what keeps people from Jesus.

> **Adam LiVecchi** ✔ @adamlivecchi
> The more we know Jesus the more confident we are in the message.

To bring people to Jesus, first we must learn to be with Him and get to know Him and then go and properly represent Him. The most dangerous sin is misrepresenting Jesus to those who don't know Him. Mark 3:14-15 states, "*And he ordained twelve, that they should be with him, and that he might send them forth to preach, and to have power to heal sicknesses, and to cast out devils.*" If you have been with Jesus, He will send you to preach or declare who He is with no apologies. Boldness to preach is directly connected to being with Jesus.

> *Then Peter, filled with the Holy Ghost, said unto them,*
> *Ye rulers of the people, and elders of Israel, if we*
> *this day be examined of the good deed done to the*

impotent man, by what means he is made whole; be it known unto you all, and to all the people of Israel, that by the name of Jesus Christ of Nazareth, whom ye crucified, whom God raised from the dead, even by him doth this man stand here before you whole. This is the stone which was set at nought of you builders, which is become the head of the corner. Neither is there salvation in any other: for there is none other name under heaven given among men, whereby we must be saved. Now when they saw the boldness of Peter and John, and perceived that they were unlearned and ignorant men, they marvelled; and they took knowledge of them, that they had been with Jesus (Acts 4:8-13).

This short story is a manifestation of Jesus ordaining people to be with Him that He might send them out to preach. Boldness to preach is just as much evidence of being filled with the Spirit as is speaking in tongues. There are people who speak in tongues all the time, but when it comes to opening their mouths about Jesus they are virtually silent. Let me encourage you to speak in tongues and boldly declare who Jesus is. If you lack boldness, spend time with Jesus and He will give you what man cannot give you. Jesus alone can make you righteous. The righteous are as bold as a lion. Let me say it like this—the righteous put full confidence in Jesus. In turn, we receive boldness from Him to declare who He is and what He has done to the world that He died for.

Jesus died for the world but lived for the church. He lived a sinless life to redeem all flesh. The message of the cross is the drawbridge into the Kingdom; remember, we preach because we were commanded to and because Jesus paid for the Father's house to be full. Our job is to invite them and compel them to come to a wedding feast, not a boring church service. The gospel is inviting people to a wedding feast, not a solemn assembly or a fast. If our message ceases to be good news, it is not the gospel.

GO. PREACH. HEAL.

Some people struggle with many different things when it comes to preaching the gospel. Often people feel unqualified to preach the gospel. Don't let the devil lie to you; the blood of Jesus is your qualifier. We must not let our past failures keep us from preaching the gospel in the here and now. As long as people are perishing we are called to preach. Peter denied Jesus three times and mere weeks later preached very powerfully and was used by God to bring many into the Kingdom. You are called and ordained. Jesus, your Commander, is your qualifier, therefore go and preach.

Questions

1. What hinders you from preaching?

    _____

    _____

    _____

2. Are you spending time to get to know the Jesus you are called to preach about?

    _____

    _____

    _____

3. Is there any person or people group specifically you feel called to preach to?

    _____

    _____

    _____

Prayer of Impartation

Father, in Jesus' name, I ask You to fill my heart with love and compassion for those You are calling me to preach to. Lord Jesus, give me courage and boldness to declare who You are. Forgive me for denying You before men by not preaching the gospel. Let preaching about You come from my knowledge of You. Holy Spirit, lead me every time I preach the gospel.

Scriptures to Meditate On

And how shall they preach, except they be sent? as it is written, How beautiful are the feet of them that preach the gospel of peace, and bring glad tidings of good things! (Romans 10:15)

Preach the word; be instant in season, out of season; reprove, rebuke, exhort with all long suffering and doctrine (2 Timothy 4:2).

For though I preach the gospel, I have nothing to glory of: for necessity is laid upon me; yea, woe is unto me, if I preach not the gospel! (1 Corinthians 9:16)

HEAL

And as ye go, preach, saying, The kingdom of heaven
is at hand. Heal the sick, cleanse the lepers, raise the
dead, cast out devils: freely ye have received,
freely give. —Matthew 10:7-8

Jesus said these words to His disciples; they were a commandment, not a suggestion. If we are His disciples, we will continue in His word. The only way we continue in His word is by obeying His commandments. Some people think they can continue in His word just by reading the Bible. That sounds nice, except it is just not true. Reading the word and praying is necessary; if I didn't do that I couldn't have written this manual. However, action or obedience is necessary for those who desire to continue in His word.

Healing is not something to be debated; it is something to be demonstrated. The body of Christ needs to stop arguing with each other and start demonstrating who Jesus Christ really is to those who don't know Him yet. That is where you come in. You are a supernatural person. We are supernatural people. The Spirit who raised Jesus from the dead lives in you, according to Romans 8:11. The Holy Spirit who took Jesus out of the grave on the third day lives in you all day, every day, and He's not going anywhere. Perhaps we are commanded to heal the sick because the Healer lives in us; just maybe, Jesus commanded us to raise the dead because He put the very Spirit who raised Him from the dead in us.

Let me tell you in plain English, Jesus believes in you and He has commanded you to be supernatural in Him. I am writing this manual to help assist this process. By Jesus commanding His disciples (or us) to heal the sick, He is actually saying to us that He has equipped us to do so. Religion says, "Wait to heal because you're not qualified." Religion says, "If it be Thy will." Yet the stripes on Jesus' back clearly reveal the will of God. Religion tries to question what God has already said. Jesus says preach the Kingdom and heal the sick. When the Kingdom is preached it actually comes. The right message creates the right atmosphere for heaven to invade earth. When the Kingdom comes, the sick are healed and demons are cast out. When the Kingdom comes, leprosy is cleansed and the dead are raised. When the Kingdom comes with power, people experience the love that God has for them. This happens when we obey Jesus and heal the sick as He commanded. The good news is people can be healed because of the stripes on Jesus' back. Bill Johnson said, "The gospel without power is simply not good news." I say amen, Bill!

Jesus didn't command us to do stuff that we can't do without Him so that we would never try. This command was an invitation to a life of power that is rooted in His love for us and His desire for people to receive the reward of His suffering. Jesus is the most unselfish person ever. He doesn't just want a reward for His suffering; He wants you and me to receive the reward of His suffering. He didn't suffer for His sin, because He didn't have any. He didn't bear stripes for His sickness, because He was never sick. His stripes were for our sicknesses that no longer belong to us because of His stripes. Everything Jesus ever did was for others.

God is maturing the body to be like the head in all things. We are partakers of His divine nature so we go and do as He did. Acts 10:38 states, "How God anointed Jesus of Nazareth with the Holy Ghost and with power: who went about doing good, and healing all that were oppressed of the devil; for God was with him." God doesn't heal people so they will love Him; He heals them because He loves them. Later we will go further into healing and some practical tips about healing the sick. However, right now I am just laying a foundation to spring forth from—a launching pad so to speak.

What we believe determines how we will live. Often people who don't have a sound mind don't have sound doctrine either. What we believe about God is what we will receive from Him. Healing is for today because Jesus Christ is the same yesterday, today, and forever. God changes not and His gospel is eternal—it transcends time, culture, and anything else. The truth of the gospel is that God loves, heals, and saves. Those who reject the gracious offer of His Son Jesus will burn in hell forever, and God will not send them an apology letter. Healing and the gospel are inseparable. What sickness is to your body, sin is to your soul. There is one remedy for both sin and sickness, and His name is Jesus Christ the Son of the living God. His blood that releases cleansing is from His stripes that release healing. When God releases forgiveness and healing we are then reconciled to Him in the way He intended us to live—both free and healed.

Adam LiVecchi ✔ @adamlivecchi
Our value for healing determines how much we really value the stripes on Jesus' back.

Our value for healing determines how much we really value the stripes on Jesus' back. The revelation of the cross is what propels our going, preaching, and healing. If we truly value Jesus' action to come to earth to seek and to save us, we will go into the entire world and seek those who are lost and sick. There comes a time when we must learn to live from what Jesus has done and not what is going on in our life, family, or nation. Our good works flow from His finished work on Calvary. Now is the time for the body of Christ to mature and bring healing to the nations.

Questions

1. Is healing part of the good news of the Kingdom?

   _____

   _____

   _____

   _____

2. Are you called to heal the sick?

   _____

   _____

   _____

   _____

3. When will you start?

   _____

   _____

   _____

   _____

Prayer of Impartation

Father, in the name of Jesus, help me to be a doer of Your word. As I obey Your word in faith, let Your Holy Spirit move mightily and bring honor to the name of Jesus. Release to me Your power and authority to heal the sick, cleanse the lepers, and raise the dead. Let me be motivated by love and moved with compassion. Release Your glory through my hands. Let me never follow signs and wonders, but let signs and wonders follow me as they follow You. Let me increase in the knowledge of God as I advance Your Kingdom through obeying Your commands. Finally, Father, strengthen me to do all this with pure motives in Jesus' name, amen.

You may feel a heat in your hands or on your body or even a fresh boldness when you are out and about. The heat is power and the boldness is authority. You don't have to feel anything to obey God. I just shared this to affirm what you may have felt, thought, or experienced. I believe the Lord Jesus imparted power and authority to you through the prayer we just prayed together, so *just do it*.

GO. PREACH. HEAL.

Scriptures to Meditate On

But he was wounded for our transgressions, he was bruised for our iniquities: the chastisement of our peace was upon him; and with his stripes we are healed (Isaiah 53:5).

And as ye go, preach, saying, The kingdom of heaven is at hand. Heal the sick, cleanse the lepers, raise the dead, cast out devils: freely ye have received, freely give (Matthew 10:7-8).

How God anointed Jesus of Nazareth with the Holy Ghost and with power: who went about doing good, and healing all that were oppressed of the devil; for God was with him (Acts 10:38).

THE FATHER'S HOUSE

Everything we receive freely in the Kingdom Jesus paid for on the tree. What revelation of the cross we have determines the understanding we operate with in the Kingdom of God. Grace isn't cheap and favor isn't free. Jesus' radical obedience to His Father earned us the favor we don't deserve and certainly can't earn or pay for. Our unmerited favor comes from the merits of Jesus' obedience and completely sinless life. James 1:14 states, "*But every man is tempted, when he is drawn away of his own lust, and enticed.*" What is awesome about this verse is it reveals something amazing about Jesus. Jesus was led into the wilderness by the Holy Spirit to be tempted by the devil. The Holy Spirit had to lead Jesus into temptation because Jesus had no lust to draw him away from the will of God. According to Isaiah 58:6, fasting looses the bonds of wickedness. Jesus had no wickedness, so the devil himself showed up. There Jesus overcame temptation. Later He tells us to pray, "*Lead us not into temptation*" (Matt. 6:13).

He teaches His disciples, and us, to pray in order to avoid being led into a battle that He has already won for us. What we need to understand about grace is that it is what Jesus has done and it is who Jesus is that causes us to be who we are and do what God has already called us to do.

Through Christ Jesus we have both a great privilege and a serious responsibility. We have the privilege because of the cross; we have a serious responsibility because the Father has a big house and He wants it to be full.

Adam LiVecchi ✔ @adamlivecchi
Everything we receive freely in the Kingdom
Jesus paid for on the tree.

🗨   🔁   ♡   ✉

*Let not your heart be troubled: ye believe in God,
believe also in me. In my Father's house are many
mansions: if it were not so, I would have told you. I go
to prepare a place for you. And if I go and prepare a
place for you, I will come again, and receive you unto
myself; that where I am, there ye may be also*
(John 14:1-3).

One day I was intently reading this scripture when the Father said
to me, "Adam, there is room for you in the Kingdom." This one phrase
really touched me in a significant way. Deep in my spirit I knew what God
was saying to me. He was revealing something to me that would leave
a responsibility upon me. The revelation was that in the Father's house
there is room for people. Jesus paid for people with His very own blood
and prepared a place for people because there was room in the Father's
house. Therefore, our hearts shouldn't be troubled or afraid.

The responsibility that God gave me was to make room for people
whom others won't. In a conversation between Jesus and me, He further
expounded to me the responsibility and benefits of making room for
others. This was what Jesus said to me in that context: "If you make room
for people whom others won't, I will show up." So I did what God had
called me to do in that capacity and the Lord's presence would come in
a strong way as I made room for others. Don't be afraid to make room

for others; don't be insecure. Remember, there is no competition in the Kingdom. Make room for others as Jesus has done for you.

Questions

1. Do you truly know the price Jesus paid for you and how valuable you are to Him?

_____

_____

_____

2. If so, how will that affect how you live your life?

_____

_____

_____

3. If the Father has room for people in His house and Jesus paid for them to be there and prepared a place for them, how are you going to bring people through Jesus to the Father so His house will be full?

_____

_____

_____

_____

_____

GO. PREACH. HEAL.

Prayer of Impartation

Father, in Jesus' name, would You show me how much Jesus paid for the lost to come home and the sick to be healed? Jesus, reveal to me how big our Father's house is. Let the Spirit of wisdom and revelation in the knowledge of who Jesus is come upon me and direct me to make room for others in the sphere of influence You have already given me.

Scriptures to Meditate On

But every man is tempted, when he is drawn away of his own lust, and enticed (James 1:14).

In my Father's house are many mansions: if it were not so, I would have told you. I go to prepare a place for you (John 14:2).

Is not this the fast that I have chosen? to loose the bands of wickedness, to undo the heavy burdens, and to let the oppressed go free, and that ye break every yoke? (Isaiah 58:6)

CHRIST IN YOU

Many people want a Savior, but very few want a Lord. Salvation is not just having a Savior but it's also having a Lord. We aren't just saved from hell; we are saved from ourselves as well if we truly allow Jesus to be our Lord. We are not just saved from something, we are saved for something! If you are a born-again believer then Christ lives within you and you live, move, and have your being in Him according to Acts 17:28. The only hope the world has for glory is the hope Christ the Father has put in you when you received what His Son Jesus did for you on the tree of Calvary. We abide in Christ for us; He abides in us for them—*them* being those who do not yet know Jesus. Some call "them" the lost, the perishing, and sinners. You get the point; remember, we used to be a "them."

In the Kingdom we don't build walls; we build bridges. Anyone can build a wall because they are easy to build, but not everyone can build a bridge. Be a bridge builder—take a risk and reach out to someone in need. Love on someone today; minister to a sick person today in Jesus' name. Go for it because Jesus believes in you.

Bill Johnson said it like this: "Jesus is in you for you, but He is upon us for them." In the Scriptures there is a difference between who we are in Christ and who Christ is in us. In Christ we are servants, disciples, friends, His brothers and sisters if we do the will of His Father. In God we are sons and daughters. Christ in us is a Savior and a Lord. What this practically means is that what Jesus says goes, and what He tells us to do we do because of who He is and what He has done for us. The gospel of John speaks about abiding in Christ and His words abiding in us. This is very interesting, especially if we look at it for what it really says and not what we want it to say or think it means. Remember, the Bible interprets the Bible. Understanding the truth of Him (Jesus) abiding in us and us abiding in Him is absolutely necessary to be fruitful in ministry.

John 14:16 states, "*And I will pray the Father, and he shall give you another Comforter, that he may abide with you for ever.*" Jesus abides in us through His Holy Spirit. John 15:4 states, "*Abide in me, and I in you. As the branch cannot bear fruit of itself, except it abide in the vine; no more can ye, except ye abide in me.*" To bear fruit we must abide in Him. That is pretty simple—even I understand it. John 15:6 says, "*If a man abide not in me, he is cast forth as a branch, and is withered; and men gather them, and cast them into the fire, and they are burned.*" There is only one kind of Christian, and they are fruitful. John 15:7 says, "*If ye abide in me, and my words abide in you, ye shall ask what ye will, and it shall be done unto you.*" When the Word abides in us, then we know what to ask for and God manifests His will through our prayers. John 15:10 states, "*If ye keep my commandments, ye shall abide in my love; even as I have kept my Father's commandments, and abide in his love.*" Jesus abides in us through His Holy Spirit, the Comforter.

If Christianity was meant to be comfortable, we would not have need of the Comforter. God doesn't love us any more or less when we obey or disobey. He so loved us while we were yet sinners that He died for us and said, "*Father, forgive them for they know not what they do*" (Luke 23:34). However, we experience His love as we obey His commands. It is only in obeying His commands that we abide in Him. You cannot abide in Him and disobey His commands; it is just not possible. The boundaries of the body of Christ are not a church building, but they are the obedience to or of His commands. The geography or boundary of His Kingdom is in the obedience to His commands. The Kingdom is where He is ruling and reigning—that rule and reign becomes manifested and visible through our obedience. So if you want to experience His love and you want to be His friend, obedience is a must.

Adam LiVecchi ✔ @adamlivecchi
When we learn to abide in Christ beyond our emotions then Jesus will overflow from our lives onto the world around us.

Some may call that legalism, but the Bible shows us friendship with God is only through obedience to His commands. John 15:14 states, *"Ye are my friends, if ye do whatsoever I command you."* When we sing *worthy is the Lamb* and don't obey Him, our worship service to God is more like a comedy hour, but it really isn't funny. There are many people singing, "I am a friend of God, He calls me friend." If we don't obey Him, He actually doesn't call us friend; He calls us lost. There are many lost Christians. If you don't believe me, just ask Jesus. What I find interesting is that there are many Christians seeking the Lord. My question is, where did He go? He actually came to seek and to save us. Then He came to live in us. What they are really trying to say is that they desire to experience the abiding presence but are not willing to obey His commands. So they spend time searching for an experience instead of focusing on obeying Him where experience is inevitable. Spend time focusing on Jesus, not seeking Him because He is not lost. In the Old Testament, people were waiting and looking for Jesus. Hebrews 12:2 states, *"Looking unto Jesus the author and finisher of our faith; who for the joy that was set before him endured the cross, despising the shame, and is set down at the right hand of the throne of God."* In the New Testament, He came and now we are looking *to* Him not *for* Him.

When we learn to abide in Christ beyond our emotions, Jesus will overflow from our lives onto the world around us. Often we are like, "God, pour out Your Spirit," and He is like, "I told you rivers would flow from your innermost being, so open your mouth and I will fill it." When

God gives revelation, it is to renew our mind. In this hour we are going from a concubine visitation attitude to a habitation, abiding in Christ. Through this the bride of Christ doctrine will be our experience. The whole bridal paradigm is about covenant and commitments, not about emotions. For all my bridal friends, the Song of Solomon is not quoted one time in the New Testament.

We experience the feelings or affections of love when we walk in covenant and obey God. We are currently in an apostolic reformation, not because I said so but because God is inviting us to be reformed on the potter's wheel. Honestly, we are a little deformed, in case you haven't noticed. If the church were truly apostolic, I wouldn't have to write this manual, selah. What God is doing now is manifesting the doctrine of the priesthood of the believer. Martin Luther was used by God to bring back the doctrine of the priesthood of all believers. In our day God is manifesting that doctrine and making it experiential for a harvest. To really walk in truth, our theology must become part of our life story. If lost people on the way to hell can't experience our doctrine, then it is false. The key that opens every door is intimacy with Jesus. Abiding in Him and Him abiding in us is a work of the Holy Spirit but also a participation of our will and choices. Ministry happens every time we say yes to Jesus and obey Him. You are a son or daughter in Christ Jesus. Jesus is Lord and King in you. King Jesus will manifest His dominion through the obedience of sons and daughters. The Father's house will be full when sons and daughters abide in the Son through obeying His commands. This is possible through the Holy Spirit. So be led by the Holy Spirit today and don't let religion, compromise, or complacency give you lead poisoning.

Questions

1. How does Christ abide in you?

   _____

   _____

2. How do you abide in Christ?

   _____

   _____

3. What is the key to answered prayer and experiencing God's love?

   _____

   _____

   _____

Prayer of Impartation

Father, in Jesus' name, let me be renewed in the spirit of my mind. Let me experience Your abiding presence. Let Your grace allow me to experience the strength to love You enough to fully obey You. Let me be fruitful in every good work and let my fruit remain. Strengthen me and cause me to persevere and accomplish all that You have for me. Let my life be hidden in Christ and let others see Christ when they see me.

GO. PREACH. HEAL.

Scriptures to Meditate On

For as many as are led by the Spirit of God, they are the sons of God (Romans 8:14).

And be not conformed to this world: but be ye transformed by the renewing of your mind, that ye may prove what is that good, and acceptable, and perfect, will of God (Romans 12:2).

And be renewed in the spirit of your mind (Ephesians 4:23).

IDENTITY AND INHERITANCE

God puts His grace toward us so we can put our faith in Him. Even our faith in Jesus is an expression of His grace. John 1:12 states, *"But as many as received him, to them gave he power to become the sons of God, even to them that believe on his name."* The word for "power" in that verse means privilege, delegated influence, or jurisdiction. Here we learn that our authority is rooted in our identity as sons of God. Jesus paid for our identity on the tree. He redeemed us, He bought us, and because His blood is that of the only begotten Son of God He brought many sons to glory. One Son equals many sons into lots of glory, which is good news.

Adam LiVecchi ✔ @adamlivecchi
Identity leads to purpose and purpose leads to destiny.

Glory is the atmosphere of royalty. Identity leads to purpose and purpose leads to destiny. Our purpose and destiny was Jesus. You are predestined to be in Him in love. When you receive His love, it transforms you and you become like Him. All of creation is groaning for the manifestation of the sons of God. My opinion is that creation is groaning for us to become like the Christ who lives within us. Often in church you will hear people say, "I don't know what I am called to do." The issue is a bit deeper than that. The real issue is that they don't know who they are. When you know who you are, naturally you know what you are supposed to do. In church, there are young adults who go in circles, following fads. There are a slew of older folks searching for purpose. Without spiritual fathers there is no identity; without identity you have lots of serious issues. If you don't believe me, just look around the next time you go to church. Fathers give their sons identity. The fatherlessness in the church is similar to that in the world. If the church doesn't invade the world, the world will invade the church. As you and I respond to the voice of God in this hour, we, by the grace of God, could see a lot of things change in this generation.

Jewish people have a bar mitzvah to celebrate maturity. When Jesus was a boy He went into the temple at the age of accountability. Joseph and Mary left Jesus in the temple. They went back for Him and here is what He said to them in a rough paraphrase: "Didn't you know that I must be about My Father's business?" Let me say it like this—God expects us to know what is going on. Jesus doesn't apologize to them because He understands He's not guilty. Part of sonship is righteousness. When someone is righteous, they see clearly and know what is going on. Righteous people rightly access reality and respond correctly to the circumstances they are in. It's clear that at the age of accountability Jesus knew who His Father was. Because He knew His Father He knew what He must do; hence, "I must be about My Father's business."

It is really important that we know our Father in heaven, because when we do, we receive our inheritance and our assignment for earth. Here at the age of accountability, the Son acknowledged His Father—He confessed Him before men, so to speak. Before Jesus went into public ministry His Father affirmed Him publicly. At the age of accountability the Son confessed who His Father was. At the age of maturity the Father acknowledged and affirmed the Son audibly and publicly. Here we see what a healthy relationship is like—two people bold about one another. Sons are bold; orphans are not. One of the purest manifestations of sonship is boldness. I believe the church is going to receive an upgrade of boldness. Boldness only grows in the secret place, so be sure to spend time with the Father especially if you want to glorify the Son by living like a son. Remember, sonship has nothing to do with gender, yet it's about our position as sons and daughters of God.

The blood of Jesus speaks a better word. We are not just forgiven by the blood but we were washed and made kings and priests to the Father because of His Son, Jesus. Revelation 1:5-6 states:

> And from Jesus Christ, who is the faithful witness, and the first begotten of the dead, and the prince of the kings of the earth. Unto him that loved us, and washed us from our sins in his own blood, and hath made us kings and priests unto God and his Father; to him be glory and dominion for ever and ever. Amen.

The blood of Jesus didn't just make us sinners saved by grace; it made us kings and priests to God. You may feel like nobody. People may tell you that you are nobody, but because of the blood of Jesus you are somebody in Him. In His world you are a king and a priest. He expects glory and dominion from you. When you know who you are in Him and what you are called to do with Him, He receives glory and dominion. You extend His Kingdom and your good works give Him glory. Our identity and inheritance is all about giving Jesus what He is worthy of. The nations are His inheritance. We receive our inheritance in Him, so we can bring Him His inheritance, which are the nations. How does this happen? Good question. Kings have influence on the earth. Priests have influence in the heavens. We are called to intercession and action, petition and legislation, glory and dominion. Priests minister to the Lord; kings minister to the people. Priests keep the house of the Lord; kings keep order in the place where they are ruling. When I say ruling, I am actually talking about serving because that is what a leader in the Kingdom is—a servant who leads by example. Let me say it like this—the government is not in Washington D.C. It is on your shoulders because you are the body of Christ. Ruling and reigning in the here and now looks like loving and serving.

When John the Revelator wrote the book of Revelation he was in exile on the Island of Patmos. During that time Christians were persecuted; they were like the scum of the earth to the society they lived in, but to God they were kings and priests. We are not defined by our circumstances or the opinions of others but by the blood of Jesus. Both the priesthood and Kingdom are received by inheritance. During Bible times, either you were born into the Levitical priesthood or you were not. If you were not born into the Levitical priesthood, there was no way of getting in.

Because of His blood we are who we are by the grace of God. Both kings and priests have responsibilities. They are political and religious. Don't shy away from politics; bring the truth of God's word to the political arena. Don't forsake the assembling of the saints. Don't just go to church; be the church. We cannot just put the Kingdom into the future. We must at all costs advance it now. It is irresponsible to push our responsibility onto another generation. Now is the time to exercise our authority in humility. Jesus believes in you, so go for it.

Questions

1. What defines you?

   _____

   _____

   _____

2. As a priest, what are your responsibilities?

   _____

   _____

   _____

3. As a king, what are you responsibilities?

   _____

   _____

   _____

Prayer of Impartation

Father, would You continually reveal Jesus to me. Holy Spirit, would You remind me of what Jesus said to me and about me. Let the blood of Jesus alone give me identity. I ask that the wisdom of God would come upon me and increase daily. Especially when it comes to living with the privileges of the Kingdom and also fulfilling my responsibilities. I ask these things believing that they will be done in Jesus' name for His glory.

Scriptures to Meditate On

According as he hath chosen us in him before the foundation of the world, that we should be holy and without blame before him in love (Ephesians 1:4).

But ye are a chosen generation, a royal priesthood, an holy nation, a peculiar people; that ye should shew forth the praises of him who hath called you out of darkness into his marvellous light (1 Peter 2:9).

Behold, what manner of love the Father hath bestowed upon us, that we should be called the sons of God: therefore the world knoweth us not, because it knew him not. Beloved, now are we the sons of God, and it doth not yet appear what we shall be: but we know that, when he shall appear, we shall be like him; for we shall see him as he is. And every man that hath this hope in him purifieth himself, even as he is pure (1 John 3:1-3).

RECONCILIATION

Therefore if any man be in Christ, he is a new creature: old things are passed away; behold, all things are become new. And all things are of God, who hath reconciled us to himself by Jesus Christ, and hath given to us the ministry of reconciliation; to wit, that God was in Christ, reconciling the world unto himself, not imputing their trespasses unto them; and hath committed unto us the word of reconciliation.
—2 Corinthians 5:17-19

Jesus has given us the ministry of reconciliation. You don't have to earn it and you don't deserve it. When the Father gave Jesus to us, we received the ministry of reconciliation because God the Father was reconciling the world to Himself in Christ. If this next session gets a hold of you and takes root on good ground perhaps you will find exactly why you are still on this planet. To properly receive the ministry of reconciliation and faithfully steward it we must let the past pass away.

Most Christians live in bondage to the past and in fear of the future. Unfortunately, with that kind of posture we open ourselves up for the devil to come in and plunder our lives, families, churches, and cities. My pastor friend Rodney Middleton from Baltimore, Maryland recently said to me in a phone conversation, "Because of the blood of Jesus, your past didn't happen." This is really powerful. Christians need to get a hold of what the blood of Jesus has truly done. The blood must come back to the forefront again. If you have believed on Jesus, forget about your past because He did. If you are operating with the mind of Christ you are not able to remember your past that is covered under the blood because He forgot about it.

Adam LiVecchi ✔ @adamlivecchi
To properly receive the ministry of reconciliation and faithfully steward it we must let the past pass away.

Jesus reconciled us to God, not counting our trespasses against us. He didn't deny the trespasses; He just covered them in His own blood reconciling us back to God. He gave us beauty for ashes, which is not a bad deal. Another word for reconciliation is *restoration*. God is the greatest restorer. With ashes He can paint a Picasso. When Jesus died for us, it wasn't just so we can go to heaven when we die; it's also so that we don't just live for ourselves anymore but for Him. When we live in that way, naturally we are ambassadors of reconciliation. Jesus said it like this: *"Blessed are the peacemakers: for they shall be called the children of God"* (Matt. 5:9). Again and again in Scripture we see identity-driven purpose because of the blood of Jesus. Because we are children of God we are peacemakers. Because we have been reconciled we have a ministry of reconciliation. Through what Jesus has done we receive identity and have a purpose. Your mission, should you choose to accept it, is to *"destroy the works of the devil"* (1 John 3:8).

Before the fall of man in the Garden of Eden, man walked with God and had a very specific and clearly defined purpose. God gave man all the resources and abilities he needed to fulfill that purpose. Man chose to disobey, which gave birth to sin and death. Jesus never sinned; He came, died, and rose again while restoring us to the place of relationship with God and purpose in the Kingdom. Our job is to bring Jesus to people and to bring people to Jesus so that they too can be restored in relationship and established in purpose. God through Christ has given us everything we need to fulfill what He desires. As we seek first the Kingdom of God and His righteousness all those things that we need shall be added to us, so that we can fulfill all of God's will for our lives. Jesus said something that perfectly illustrates the ministry of reconciliation. Luke 19:10 states, *"For the Son of man is come to seek and to save that which was lost."*

Do you say yes to the mission? I take it you do. A very sobering and harsh reality is that not every lost sheep will want to come home. In the ministry of reconciliation you will want to be an agent of restoration, and some people just don't want restoration or reconciliation because it means accountability. You will experience the fellowship of Jesus' sufferings when this happens; it will be with many tears.

I can remember many times spent on my face crying out to God over these sorts of circumstances. Confessing my part that caused any brokenness, forgiving others, and praying God's best for them. One of those times the Holy Spirit whispered something to me that changed my perspective. He said, "Adam, I will not restore relationships that I have not ordained for you to have." That made me really understand that Jesus is Lord over who He permits to be in my life or not. Often people and even leaders in the body of Christ will use the excuse "the Lord told me" in order to not be accountable, but in reality it is not usually the Lord, it's their lord whose name is "self." There are people who would rather fault-find with everyone else instead of making themselves accountable to others. I can honestly tell you that I have experienced more pain and brokenness in relationships with Christians than I did when I was a heathen selling drugs and living like the devil. I have seen more betrayal and craziness among Christians than in the world. The church needs more restoration than I can fit in the nation of Russia, but God the Holy Spirit is fully committed so that is good news.

Division in the church means a lack of vision. God's vision is reconciliation, which is what the blood of Jesus paid for. It is our privilege as Kingdom ambassadors to manifest God's vision for His Son. Before the foundation of the world, God the Father, Son, and Holy Spirit were the most healthy and functional family ever. They invited the whole world of dysfunctional people into Their family that we might function properly and thrive under His leadership. God in Christ is calling the world to Himself. Jesus' enemies are being made His footstool by His friends.

Our part of the reconciliation process is to extend mercy and warn those who reject it. We plant, we water, but it is God alone who brings the increase. You are agents of change in this world, ministers of reconciliation. As such, be prepared for rejection. People will reject the notion of restoration because it isn't cheap. Through this you will have to do what God does and respect their free will and love them. God is going to teach us to love the hell out of people like He did for us. Often love hurts, but it never fails, so just keep on loving people in Jesus' name. It is Him who strengthens you, so through Him you can love even those who don't love you.

I was listening to Graham Cooke one day and he was telling a story about a man who didn't like him and thought he was a false prophet. The guy said to Graham, "I don't like you; you are my enemy." Graham replied, "You are not my enemy. I won't let you be my enemy. I really like you." The guy just broke down and cried. We must choose to never let how other people feel about us define how we feel about them. The concept of reconciliation that Paul the apostle wrote about was Jesus reconciling the world to Himself. So much of the world has successfully invaded the church and much of the church needs to be reconciled to Jesus. Now is the time for the church to invade the world with the ministry of reconciliation.

Questions

1. What would the ministry of reconciliation look like in your context?

   _____

   _____

2. If I am more focused on what you did to me than what I did to you, is that a recipe for reconciliation?

   _____

   _____

3. What do you do if someone rejects the notion of restoration?

   _____

   _____

   _____

Prayer of Impartation

Father, in Christ You have already made me a minister or servant of reconciliation. I have been made an ambassador, not a diplomat. Let me function in the ministry You have given me faithfully. I declare that I am a peacemaker. Let me be strong and very courageous as I extend Your grace and mercy to others. I pray this in the name of Jesus Christ, Son of the living God.

GO. PREACH. HEAL.

Scriptures to Meditate On

And I will restore to you the years that the locust hath eaten, the cankerworm, and the caterpiller, and the palmerworm, my great army which I sent among you (Joel 2:25).

And that he died for all, that they which live should not henceforth live unto themselves, but unto him which died for them, and rose again (2 Corinthians 5:15).

Brethren, if a man be overtaken in a fault, ye which are spiritual, restore such an one in the spirit of meekness; considering thyself, lest thou also be tempted. Bear ye one another's burdens, and so fulfil the law of Christ (Galatians 6:1-2).

GROWING IN FAITH

Often people want to grow in faith but don't want to learn to listen. Remember, faith comes by hearing, and before hearing or understanding there is listening. James 1:19 states, "*Wherefore, my beloved brethren, let every man be swift to hear, slow to speak, slow to wrath.*" James writes this because often we are not quick to listen. Often people who are quick to speak are quick to get angry as well. Anger and bitterness are completely contrary to faith. One of the most mature expressions of faith is forgiveness. Listening is a learned behavior; it doesn't come to most people naturally. Growing in faith is not just about the miraculous; it is also about growing in the area of convictions. Biblical faith will cause us to be people of integrity. Conviction must give birth to integrity or we are hypocrites. You can have all of the faith in the world, but if you have no integrity it means nothing. Biblical faith should cause us to live uprightly and have a clear conscience. Faith operates best through love, a clear conscience, and pure motives.

To grow in faith, we must first be established in the faith. Here are a few verses to help us understand how authentic faith comes and is established.

> So then faith cometh by hearing, and hearing by the word of God (Romans 10:17).

> And my speech and my preaching was not with enticing words of man's wisdom, but in demonstration of the

Spirit and of power: that your faith should not stand in the wisdom of men, but in the power of God (1 Corinthians 2:4-5).

Adam LiVecchi ✔ @adamlivecchi
Faith operates best through love, a clear conscience, and pure motives.

Here we learn that faith comes by hearing the word of God and faith stands in the power of God. Paul the apostle, under the influence of the Holy Spirit, penned both of these scriptures. Everything Paul wrote is rooted in Christ Jesus; there is no truth apart from Him. If you can't show it to me in Jesus, my eyes don't have much interest in it. If we go to John 2 we will find Jesus and His disciples at a wedding in Cana of Galilee. At the wedding they ran out of wine, which means perhaps the people who were getting married weren't rich. Rich people usually don't run out of wine—just a thought. Anyway, Mary comes to Jesus telling Him about the problem, and He tells her it is not His hour or it is not God's timing. She turns to the servants and tells them to do whatever Jesus says. That right there is the key to biblical faith—do whatever Jesus says. The miraculous is activated when we act in faith. Another way to say it would be the obedience of faith activates the miraculous. The miraculous is a manifestation of God's glory. At the end of this wedding story it says in John 2:11, *"This beginning of miracles did Jesus in Cana of Galilee, and manifested forth his glory; and his disciples believed on him."* Their faith was standing in His power. An authentic gospel will produce real disciples.

To grow in faith you must walk by faith. In the Kingdom, shortcuts do not exist. To really know something you must experience it. Any honest New Testament Greek scholar will admit this is true. In the Greek language there is "to know" by *knowledge* and another "to know" by *experience*. Walking by faith cannot be attained by knowing with your head or heart. Your feet must get involved as well. Second Corinthians 5:7 states, *"For we walk by faith, not by sight."* Sometimes truth needs to be seen. In the Gospels there is a great story that illustrates this truth perfectly. Jesus was walking on the water and the disciples were really scared. Peter said, "Lord, if it is You call me out there." Jesus responded with one word: "Come." When Peter got out of the boat, he began to walk by faith. When he started to walk by sight, immediately he began to sink. The good news is that Jesus reached out and picked him up, and together they walked on water back to the ship. So faith came to Peter by him hearing the voice of Jesus. His faith stood on the water literally in the power of God, and he began to walk by faith. This is a clear picture of how we grow in faith. God speaks and faith is released; we respond in faith, and God's power is experienced. Then we become His followers as we walk by faith.

When God speaks, we are strengthened and built up. When others prophesy a true word from the Lord, we are edified. When the word of God is preached, we grow in faith. So God and others are essential in the growth of our faith. In First Corinthians 12, Paul the apostle writes about the gift of faith. Faith is an awesome gift. Often it comes wrapped in the midst of circumstances that are less than favorable. There is also a role only you can play in the building up of your faith. Jude 1:20-21 states:

> But ye, beloved, building up yourselves on your most holy faith, praying in the Holy Ghost, keep yourselves in the love of God, looking for the mercy of our Lord Jesus Christ unto eternal life.

Your most holy faith is built up when you pray in the Holy Spirit or in tongues. When your spirit communicates directly to God's in a way that surpasses your understanding, your most holy faith is built up. This may be the very reason that by faith we understand. First we believe, then we understand. Most people want to understand and then believe, but that is not faith. When faith grows up, it turns into trust. Faith is like a tiny mustard seed; faith can move a mountain. Trust is with all of your heart and it will move you. Walking by faith is to mature us to the place of trust. When we fully trust God we don't question His integrity with our unbelief. Trust is the complete absence of unbelief, and that is where the Holy Spirit wants to take the body of Christ because that is who Jesus is. Jesus' will was perfect, yet He laid it down in full surrender, which is what God is looking for. He wants us to be wholly given, fully yielded, and all in. We must let faith grow into trust in our lives. When it does you won't be worried about what God is already fully in control of. It is a very freeing place to be. Jesus spent all of His time there, and He is calling us to be where He is. Together we are on an amazing journey with the most amazing guide ever. The Holy Spirit is fully committed to us growing up in faith until we look like Christ Jesus.

For those of you who are really hungry to minister Christ to the world, you are going to have to learn to forgive the church. When Jesus was on the tree He screamed, "Father, forgive them for they know not what they do!" The Father desires that kind of faith. The writer of Hebrews tells us, *"Without faith it is impossible to please him"* (Heb. 11:6). Faith in God means that we are not victims to what others have said about us or done to us. Instead of being victims, we are conquers through forgiveness. Often the people that you will need to forgive won't apologize. It is almost like a Christian book; most of the people who really need the book won't buy it because mostly they are unaware of their need. There are others who are blatantly defiant and won't acknowledge their need, but leave it to God—He has an amazing way of sorting all that stuff out.

When we are humble, we become much more aware of our need. Humility is a virtue that allows us to see spiritually. The proud are spiritually blind. I have been there, so I know by experience what it is to be a first-class idiot. Humility allows us to be honest with ourselves and with others. Often presumption assumes what is not true—this also can be called deception. Deception is the very opposite of faith because real faith is only rooted in truth. The disciples walked with Jesus for three years. Peter walked on water. God multiplied food through their hands. They experienced water being turned to wine. They healed the sick and cast out demons. They saw the dead raised through the voice of Jesus. Only once does Scripture record them asking for an increase of faith.

> Then said he unto the disciples, It is impossible but that offences will come: but woe unto him, through whom they come! It were better for him that a millstone were hanged about his neck, and he cast into the sea, than that he should offend one of these little ones. Take heed to yourselves: If thy brother trespass against thee, rebuke him; and if he repent, forgive him. And if he trespass against thee seven times in a day, and seven times in a day turn again to thee, saying, I repent; thou shalt forgive him. And the apostles said unto the Lord, Increase our faith (Luke 17:1-5).

They needed more faith to stay in relationship with one another. In the body of Christ, there are a lot of broken relationships due to a lack of biblical faith. Jesus said if you don't forgive you won't be forgiven. Faith forgives before someone apologizes. Mature Christians don't focus on what has happened to them. Mature Christians focus on what Jesus did and forgive just like He did. We have to make the decision to forgive before we are wronged. Will you choose to forgive people for what they have done? Will you chose to forgive others for what they will do?

I want to share a very powerful story of forgiveness. (This was before I was a Christian.) My friends and I were getting high, doing and selling drugs in a small town in New Jersey. It was a hot summer night. We were on ecstasy and we were drinking brandy and smoking a lot of weed. We were probably all lucky just to be alive. One of my friends owed my other friend a thousand dollars. The debtor kept instigating and talking crazy to my other friend. To make a long story short, they began to fight. Very quickly the lender put his knees on the shoulders of the debtor and was literally smashing his head against cement. All you could hear was *bang, bang*, and high-pitched screams.

My conscience was seared with a hot iron, so I didn't do anything about what was happening. I was beginning to have no regard for human life. I was thinking more about what we would do with a dead body, even though the debtor was my friend as well. Then one of our friends, a true peacemaking, drunken Good Samaritan, jumped in and stopped what could have been a young man's death.

During those days, I had the nicest car out of all of my friends, which means I drove most of the time. To get to the point, about thirty minutes later the debtor and the lender who were just fighting were in the car together and were friends again. Since then, the lender, who was my best friend growing up, died. The debtor was quick to forgive. Now he is a father, a husband, and has a successful business in New Jersey.

This story of forgiveness touches me deeply every time I think of it. I have seen church people hold grudges for years for much less than a head being smashed against cement. When the church is less forgiving than drug dealers, it is clear we have a serious problem. I hope your faith in Christ will encourage you to let go of any hard feelings that you may have toward anyone. When faith is on the offensive it preaches, heals, and demonstrates the Kingdom. When faith is on the defensive it forgives, shows mercy, and prays for those who talk about you. Remember, faith is a shield and it protects us from unbelief, the lies of the devil, the opinions of others, and unforgiveness. For your faith to grow it must be challenged and tried. The trial of your faith is necessary for the growth of your faith. The trial of your faith is precious. It may not feel good, but it will cause growth if you respond correctly.

Questions

1. What is the difference between faith and presumption?

   _____

   _____

   _____

2. Who in your life is God using to help you consistently grow in your faith?

   _____

   _____

   _____

3. What would be some manifestations of you growing in faith?

   _____

   _____

   _____

Prayer of Impartation

Father, would You release the gift of faith in me. I ask that I would be attentive to Your voice so that I will be built up in faith. Cause me to be a good listener and a faithful follower. Let me be a person of strong and unwavering convictions that are lived out with integrity. I ask these things in Jesus' name.

Scriptures to Meditate On

For therein is the righteousness of God revealed from faith to faith: as it is written, The just shall live by faith (Romans 1:17).

Examine yourselves, whether ye be in the faith; prove your own selves. Know ye not your own selves, how that Jesus Christ is in you, except ye be reprobates? (2 Corinthians 13:5)

For whatsoever is born of God overcometh the world: and this is the victory that overcometh the world, even our faith (1 John 5:4).

UNCOVERING A POPULAR LIE

Often in church you hear some pretty bizarre things. For the sake of learning I am going to share one with you. Unfortunately this statement came from supposedly mature believers or even "on fire young people." Here, a filthy lie is about to be uprooted, so put your seat belt on.

"I am not called to evangelism."

Adam LiVecchi ✔ @adamlivecchi
If the gates of hell are prevailing, it is not the church.

🗨   ♺   ♡   ✉

I have heard supposedly Spirit-filled Christians say this very phrase. They are filled with a spirit and it is not holy. It is actually a spirit of fear. Here the spirit of fear and the fear of man work together to silence the church. However, the real church cannot be silenced. Let me say it like this—if the gates of hell are prevailing, it is not the church. The gates of hell not prevailing against the church means the Kingdom of God advances at all times no matter what, hence, *"Of the increase of his government and peace there shall be no end"* (Isa. 9:7). The gates of hell not prevailing means that we plunder the enemy's camp and take back the people he has trapped in darkness. The Kingdom of God is not defensive. It is always offensive and it only moves forward. When Paul the apostle wrote about the armor of the Lord in Ephesians 6 there was no armor for the back of the soldier because forward is the only option in the Kingdom.

Jesus told His disciples to pray that the Lord of the harvest send forth laborers into His harvest, and then He sent them out to preach and demonstrate the Kingdom. If we are going to know and follow the Lord of the harvest then we are going to have to get into His harvest field. When Jesus said, "The fields are ripe unto harvest," He really meant it (see John 4:35).

When Jesus commanded His disciples to go into the world, He really meant it, and He has never changed His mind. Jesus actually believes that when we go, His presence will be with us to reveal who He is. Jesus believes that our light shining is directly connected to the Father receiving glory. Let me say it like this—you are called to win souls and you are called and chosen, so be faithful. Faithful means moving forward and not looking back. Luke 9:62 states, *"And Jesus said unto him, No man, having put his hand to the plough, and looking back, is fit for the kingdom of God."* Those who are fit for the Kingdom don't have time to look back because they are moving forward. If you are going to move forward in the Kingdom, you must pick up the plow and get your hands dirty in the Lord's harvest field. Whether you are a housewife, an intercessor, a worship leader, a schoolteacher, or a computer technician, you are called to the harvest field.

Let us consider some very sobering words. Luke 11:23 states, *"He that is not with me is against me: and he that gathereth not with me scattereth."* By not choosing Jesus, people are actually opposing Him. By not gathering people into His Kingdom, people are actually working directly against Him. These are serious and indicting words; they are very strong and uncomfortable. Just because these words are uncomfortable doesn't mean we should ignore them. As a matter of fact, if you want to grow spiritually you must get out of your comfort zone so the Holy Spirit can be your Comforter as you go through spiritual growing pains, so to speak.

5 Hindrances to Evangelizing

1. A lie that has said, "You are not called to evangelism."

2. The spirit of fear and/or the fear of man.

3. Selfishness that causes people to be silent when they need to speak.

4. Leaders who don't train their own people how to actually evangelize and then lead by example. (Leaders, remember your people will not do what you say, they will do what you do. In the Kingdom all leadership is by example.)

5. Unbelief that God will actually use them. (My dad, Angelo LiVecchi, suggested this one.)

Questions

1. What helps when people learn to do evangelism effectively?

   _____

   _____

2. What does effective evangelism look like, biblically speaking?

   _____

   _____

3. Are you being held back from sharing your faith and demonstrating who Jesus is?

   _____

   _____

4. If so, what exactly is holding you back? Ask the Holy Spirit to reveal this to you. Wait on Him; write down what He says or the thoughts that go through your mind. After you write them down, pray and make confession. Then see if an opportunity arises for you to step out in faith; if one doesn't arise, create one.

   _____

   _____

   _____

   _____

Prayer of Impartation

Father, in Jesus' name, free me now from the spirit of fear and the fear of man. Give me boldness to preach and demonstrate who Your Son Jesus really is. Lord, forgive me for being selfish and complacent when it comes to obeying You when You commanded us to go, preach, and heal. Jesus, I want to know You and make You known. Help me to move forward with You and never look back. Thank You for hearing me, Father.

Scriptures to Meditate On

And Jesus said unto him, No man, having put his hand to the plough, and looking back, is fit for the kingdom of God (Luke 9:62).

He that is not with me is against me: and he that gathereth not with me scattereth (Luke 11:23).

The fruit of the righteous is a tree of life; and he that winneth souls is wise (Proverbs 11:30).

GIVE. PRAY. FAST.

Unfortunately, many believers today relate to Jesus like what He says to do is optional. Often we pick and choose what is convenient or beneficial for us when it comes to obeying Christ. This must change, especially if we call Jesus Lord and really desire for Jesus to be Lord of our lives. The truth is that Jesus is Lord, but is that true in the decisions we make and the life we live? I know you want to call Jesus Lord and live like you mean it. From that place of understanding, I write the "whens" of biblical Christianity.

In Matthew 5, Jesus turned His disciples' world upside down. He repeated these two phrases many times in the Sermon on the Mount (Matt. 5–7): "*It hath been said*" and "*But I say unto you.*" He taught them what "hath been said," which was past tense; then He taught them what they needed to know: "but I say unto you," present tense. If you want to live in God's presence you must live in the present moment. When Jesus ministered He said, "Repent, the Kingdom of God is at hand." What He is saying is the time for God to manifest His dominion is now. He taught them a whole new way of life. The way we follow Jesus is by obeying His commandments; if we think that we follow Jesus any other way, we are deceived. Jesus teaches us in Matthew 6 the "whens" of Kingdom life. They are as follows:

1. Matthew 6:2: "*Therefore when thou doest thine alms, do not sound a trumpet before thee, as the hypocrites do in the synagogues and in the streets, that they may*

have glory of men. Verily I say unto you, They have their reward."

2. Matthew 6:5: *"And when thou prayest, thou shalt not be as the hypocrites are: for they love to pray standing in the synagogues and in the corners of the streets, that they may be seen of men. Verily I say unto you, They have their reward."*

3. Matthew 6:16: *"Moreover when ye fast, be not, as the hypocrites, of a sad countenance: for they disfigure their faces, that they may appear unto men to fast. Verily I say unto you, They have their reward."*

Jesus didn't say *if* you fast, if you give, or *if* you pray; He said *when*. To some people this sounds radical, but to a Jewish person in the days of Jesus it would be normal. The deeper issue that Jesus and grace address here is the motivation of the heart. The law says do not commit adultery. Jesus and grace say that if you look on a woman to lust you have already committed adultery. The standard isn't only about action; it is about thoughts and intentions because now we have been given the mind of Christ. The mind of Christ makes ministry easy if we don't lean on our own understanding. In the verses above, Jesus is telling His disciples don't do the right things for the wrong reasons because if you do you'll have your reward and that reward is a counterfeit of the real reward your Father in heaven wants to give you.

Fasting, praying, and giving are necessary parts of the Christian's life. They are the privileges of discipline. For them to serve their true purpose, they must be done with the right motives. In a religious culture, fasting and praying becomes like peer pressure instead of Spirit-led and for the Father's eyes only. I understand the purpose of corporate prayer and fasting; however, I am addressing what Jesus addressed and that is why we do what we do and who we do it for. Hebrews 4:12 states:

For the word of God is quick, and powerful, and sharper than any twoedged sword, piercing even to the dividing asunder of soul and spirit, and of the joints and marrow, and is a discerner of the thoughts and intents of the heart.

The word of God is a discerner of the thoughts and the intentions. The word of God discerns what you think and why you think it. The word, which is Jesus, is a discerner. Jesus actually is the One who gives us discernment through the Holy Spirit. In the Kingdom, motives mean as much as actions. We must ask the Lord to purify our motives even when we are doing the right things.

When we are immature, the Lord will deal with our actions. As we mature, He deals more with our motives and intentions. Now is the time when God is maturing His people, and spiritual disciplines are one of the ways He brings about maturity in the life of believers. As we mature, we come to see that spiritual disciplines are actually a privilege, not a burden. I will give you a brief example in the natural. Someone who lives in a democratic republic may see their mortgage payment as a burden, but someone in a communist country or someone who lives under a dictator would see owning their own home as a privilege they wish they could have. Perspective is everything. If you live with a half empty cup, you won't share any of your water for fear of not having enough. If you live from the perspective of the cup being half full, then you will share your water with someone who has no water.

The revelation of the goodness of God makes us want to share Him with others. People who don't really share Jesus with others don't really believe He is good enough to share. When a shift in perspective comes, then there will be a shift in our motives and actions. Spiritual maturity is about a shift in perspective; it is about seeing through the eyes of Jesus because we have been given the mind of Christ. The three spiritual disciplines of giving, praying, and fasting help the maturity process because we become less and less selfish as we do those things with the right motives.

I personally find the order these three "whens" fall in very interesting. They are as follows—give, pray, fast. If you expect to receive something from God, give something to someone. Luke 16:11-12 states:

> If therefore ye have not been faithful in the unrighteous mammon, who will commit to your trust the true riches? And if ye have not been faithful in that which is another man's, who shall give you that which is your own?

By being faithful and by giving in the natural, we show God that we are ready to receive something of the supernatural. By giving what we have, we receive that which money cannot buy. In the Kingdom to receive you must give, to be exalted you must humble yourself. Things work a little differently in the Kingdom, and we must learn the ways of the King if we want to represent Him properly. Giving to the poor or the giving of alms, praying, and fasting are all ministries to the Lord. Before we minister to people we minister to the Lord. It is the first and greatest commandment that gives us fuel for the second commandment, which is expressed through the great commission. First things must be first. Giving, praying, and fasting are disciplines that will cause you to persevere. Perseverance is patience in motion.

It is important to understand that ministering to the Lord is not for people to see you but for you to get to really know your heavenly Father who desires to spend time with His children in the secret place. To live a life hidden in Christ, doing the right things for the right reasons is essential, especially when it comes to living out the Christian life before people. If we live to please anyone but God we will find ourselves in compromise. Giving, praying, and fasting are things we do in the natural to keep our spiritual life aligned with God's purposes. It is not about a rigid schedule of exactly when to do them or how often we do them; it is about having a heart that says my Father watches and waits in secret and above all things I want to please Him. To know God you must spend time with Him; there are no shortcuts in relationship.

Questions

1. Is giving to the poor, praying, and fasting a part of your life?

   _____

2. Have you found yourself doing the right things for the wrong reasons?

   _____

3. Do you see Jesus' intentions when He commanded us to give, pray, and fast?

   _____

   _____

Prayer of Impartation

Father, would You show me Jesus' intentions when He commanded us to give to the poor, pray, and fast. Help me to understand Your heart and desire to be close to me. Help us to abide in You and keep Your commands. Teach us these disciplines so we don't need unnecessary discipline. Help us to do the right things for the right reasons. In Jesus' name we pray.

GO. PREACH. HEAL.

Scriptures to Meditate On

Therefore when thou doest thine alms, do not sound a trumpet before thee, as the hypocrites do in the synagogues and in the streets, that they may have glory of men. Verily I say unto you, They have their reward (Matthew 6:2).

And when thou prayest, thou shalt not be as the hypocrites are: for they love to pray standing in the synagogues and in the corners of the streets, that they may be seen of men. Verily I say unto you, They have their reward (Matthew 6:5).

Moreover when ye fast, be not, as the hypocrites, of a sad countenance: for they disfigure their faces, that they may appear unto men to fast. Verily I say unto you, They have their reward (Matthew 6:16).

THE SECRET PLACE

He that dwelleth in the secret place of the most High
shall abide under the shadow of the Almighty.
—Psalm 91:1

The word *secret place* in this verse also means protection, and in ministry you will need that for sure. The shadow of His wings is near to His heart; it is the place where He is our covering, but that is another message for another book. Jesus, in the New Testament, defined the secret place as a place where the Father looks and waits. In His discourse before His death in the book of John He talks about abiding in Him. From Matthew 5 to John 15, there is a great progression of revelation that we need to understand if we want to release pure ministry. The secret place goes from a place we visit to a place we live or abide in. The secret place is also what we take with us when we leave our house and go about our normal life. I will share a few examples about this and one very personal experience.

The secret place is not merely a prayer closet, but it certainly begins there. The disciples knew the secret to Jesus' ministry, which is why they asked, "Lord teach us to pray." The time that Jesus spent in secret with His Father was what shaped His public ministry. Remember, what you do in secret will be rewarded openly. One of the first things I realized in ministry was that no demon or religious controlling leader could ever get in the way of what my Father desired to give me. We must live from the secret place and not for people's approval. We must live for the Father's good pleasure, not to please people. Often if you live to please God, people won't always be happy with you, but at the end of the day it's what Jesus says that really matters. When you live to please God, godly people will support that which God has established in you. Secure people will affirm that which they cannot control. Insecure people will dismiss what they cannot control. Jesus was under the authority but completely out of the control of men; this is where the Father desires us to be. Does He want us to be accountable to people? Yes! Does He want us to be under their control? No way. The more you spend time with the Lord, the more you will want to do things His way and be accountable to people. It is through accountability that integrity is built. Ministry can be sustainable when we become accountable.

Adam LiVecchi ● @adamlivecchi
Ministry can be sustainable when we become accountable.

Here is a prophetic word for you. What you do in secret will be rewarded openly. David is a great example of this truth. Behind the scenes he killed a lion and a bear. On the front lines, he killed a giant named Goliath. Both times he was looking after his father's sheep. Both times he had someone else's best interests at heart. We do the greatest exploits when we are about the interests of others. What David did in secret was rewarded in the open. On the backside of the mountain David sang the high praises of God. When he came in from battle, Israel sang his praises when they sang, "*Saul hath slain his thousands, and David his ten thousands*" (1 Sam. 18:7).

Corporate prayer, praise, and worship is not the secret place. The presence of the Lord may come during worship. However, usually what we feel is the anointing, but in reality the secret place is a place of solitude; it is the place when we are alone with the Lord. Corporate worship is awesome and necessary, but it doesn't replace the secret place. In the same way, the secret place doesn't replace corporate worship; it is not one or the other. It is both. Your personal history with God develops in the secret place. The secret place is where we become pregnant with promise; it is in the secret place where we give birth to the purposes of God. Daniel 3:22-27 states:

> Therefore because the king's commandment was urgent, and the furnace exceeding hot, the flames of the fire slew those men that took up Shadrach, Meshach, and Abednego. And these three men, Shadrach, Meshach, and Abednego, fell down bound into the midst of the burning fiery furnace. Then Nebuchadnezzar the king was astonished, and rose up in haste, and spake, and said unto his counsellors, Did not we cast three men bound into the midst of the fire? They answered and said unto the king, True, O king. He answered and said, Lo, I see four men loose, walking in the midst of the fire, and they have no hurt; and the form of the fourth is like the Son of God. Then Nebuchadnezzar came near to the mouth of the burning fiery furnace, and spake, and said, Shadrach, Meshach, and Abednego, ye servants of the most high God, come forth, and come hither. Then Shadrach, Meshach, and Abednego, came forth of the midst of the fire. And the princes, governors, and captains, and the king's counsellors, being gathered together, saw these men, upon whose bodies the fire had no power, nor was an hair of their head singed, neither were their

coats changed, nor the smell of fire had passed on them.

The secret place is a Person, and His name is Jesus. When He showed up in the fire, it could not burn them. When He showed up, their chains fell off and they were free. Shadrach, Meshach, and Abednego were in the secret place; therefore, fire could not burn them. The secret place is a place of divine protection. When lions couldn't eat Daniel, it was because he was under the shadow of His wings in the secret place. A crowd of people wanted to grab Jesus and throw Him off a mountain, yet He managed to walk through the crowd untouched. He was abiding in the secret place. Tradition says that John the Revelator was thrown in boiling oil to be burned alive, twice. The oil could not burn his physical body because he was in the secret place. Paul was hidden away for three years. The secret place empowered him to become one of the most powerful apostolic ministers the world has ever seen. God has been hiding you to reveal His Son in you.

The secret place is my favorite place to be. Spending time with my Abba is my absolute favorite activity. That communion and communication with Him is what I live for and from. Everything else flows from that place.

The secret place is not about seeking the Lord; it is about spending time with Him. He came to seek and save us—the real issue is not about seeking the Lord, but rather focusing on Him. The Father is waiting in the secret place; He watches and waits for us. The secret place is a very personal message to me. When the earthquake shook Haiti on January 12, 2010, I was there in the very epicenter of the quake—Carrefour, Haiti. Christina Stewart of Impact Nations and I were in Haiti ministering and planning a journey of compassion for that summer. We were staying with Pastor Eddy François and his wife Marlene. On January 12, 2010 she cooked an amazing Haitian lunch. It was so good it put me to sleep. When the earth began to violently shake, I was sleeping. When I heard the first boom, I saw the cinderblock wall to my left split like a piece of paper being ripped. I, by the grace of God, immediately popped up out of the bed. When I got up, the cinderblock wall that my bed was on imploded and wound up crushing the bed I was sleeping on. I was living in the secret place—the place of protection.

Adam LiVecchi ✔ @adamlivecchi
The secret place is not about seeking the Lord; it is about spending time with Him.

God divinely protected me and preserved me. I was covered under the shadow of His wings. When I could not protect myself, His glory was my rear guard. He was watching over His word to perform it. My life was completely in His hands and there was nothing I did to save myself. He woke me up and lifted me out of my sleep immediately guiding me through the house while the cinderblock roof was collapsing. I write this with tears in my eyes at 3:39 in the morning, remembering the faithfulness of the God I am writing about. Truly there is no one like Jesus.

Often in prayer we come to such a special place of intimate connection with the Father. When I was sleeping, He was at such an intimate place with me that He woke me up and led me out safely. I ran through the house screaming for Christina, got her, then my friend Jordan Amboise helped us get out of the house. About 300,000 people were not that fortunate that day. I am very grateful to be alive.

This last part was about my history with God. I share this to stir your faith and to encourage you that God is looking out for you even if you may not be fully aware of it. He is watching over you and protecting you. Your life is fully in His hands. You just need to trust Him. Living from the secret place will always produce testimonies. So abide in Jesus and let His words abide in you.

Questions

1. Do you set aside time to spend with the Father in the secret place?

   _____

   _____

2. Will you set aside time daily to spend with your Father?

   _____

   _____

3. If you don't spend time with the Father daily, what do you think your life will look like in five years? What will happen if you do spend time with Him?

   _____

   _____

   _____

Prayer of Impartation

Father, in Jesus' name, would You release a supernatural hunger and a desire to know You. Let my main priority be to get to know You intimately and walk with You faithfully. I thank You for the secret place and the open reward You have for me in Christ. Like Jesus knew His Abba, let me know You in that same manner. Father, it is in Jesus' name that I ask all these things.

Scriptures to Meditate On

He that dwelleth in the secret place of the most High shall abide under the shadow of the Almighty (Psalm 91:1).

He shall cover thee with his feathers, and under his wings shalt thou trust: his truth shall be thy shield and buckler (Psalm 91:4).

The secret of the Lord is with them that fear him; and he will shew them his covenant (Psalm 25:14).

A LIFE-CHANGING PRAYER

To really know God you must read His word and pray. Spending time in worship and waiting to hear God's voice is essential if you truly want to know God for yourself. God is the most misrepresented Person ever; if you don't believe me, ask Him. All public ministry is conceived in private. The first commandment fuels the second commandment. The great commission—which is to go into all the world, preach the gospel, and make disciples by teaching them to observe all the things that Jesus has commanded—is one of the primary expressions of truly loving your neighbor. We love God because He first loved us. The more that truth sets in our hearts, the more it is expressed through our lives. The disciples truly understood the secret to Jesus' ministry, which is why they asked Him, "Teach us to pray." The good news is, He did teach His disciples and us to pray.

Through reading and spending time with Jesus, He revealed something to me. Here it is in a nutshell. It is wisdom that makes power and favor sustainable. I turned something that happened to Jesus in Scripture into a prayer by the leading of the Holy Spirit. This prayer has totally changed my life and is still changing my life and ministry. Luke 2:52 states, "*And Jesus increased in wisdom and stature, and in favour with God and man.*" Here Jesus increased because His Kingdom increased; hence "*Of the increase of his government and peace there shall be no end*" (Isa. 9:7).

He increased in three specific areas. Focusing on these areas is key if we are going to live out the will of God for our lives. Remember, Jesus is the will of God, and He is our example in all things. If He, being God in the flesh, needed to increase in three specific areas, we obviously do too. He increased in wisdom, favor, and stature.

> **Adam LiVecchi** ✔ @adamlivecchi
> We need to increase in wisdom so we will know what to do with favor.

Now for the life-changing prayer:

Father, I thank You that I am increasing in wisdom, stature, and in favor with You, Father, and with men, just as Jesus did.

We need to increase in wisdom so we will know what to do with favor. Wisdom makes favor sustainable. As this happens we increase in stature or maturity. In the Greek, the word used for "stature" means age and maturity. In reality, some people get older but spiritually they don't mature and assume responsibility for what God called them to do. Maturity means responsibility. I believe that you are one of those who will mature and increase in wisdom and in favor with God and man. Please pray that prayer sincerely and diligently for a year and send me an e-mail letting me know what increase God has brought to your life, family, church, ministry, or business.

E-mail us at info@weseejesusministries.com

In the subject write "Luke 2:52 prayer"

We look forward to hearing the good things that God will do. Just remember, this prayer is dangerous. If you are praying it, expect changes in your life. Expect the exceedingly, abundantly more than you can ask, think, or imagine from God.

Questions

1. When was the last time you asked God for wisdom?

   _____

   _____

2. If you were filled with wisdom, what would your life look like?

   _____

   _____

3. What are three ways to get wisdom?

   _____

   _____

   _____

Prayer of Impartation

Father, I ask You to give me supernatural wisdom. Let Your wisdom cause me to be a faithful steward of all You do, say, and give me. I ask this in Jesus' name.

Scriptures to Meditate On

The fear of the Lord is the beginning of wisdom: a good understanding have all they that do his commandments: his praise endureth for ever (Psalm 111:10).

Get wisdom, get understanding: forget it not; neither decline from the words of my mouth (Proverbs 4:5).

Wisdom is the principal thing; therefore get wisdom: and with all thy getting get understanding (Proverbs 4:7).

WHEN FAVOR COMES

Favor comes by asking for it in prayer. It comes in spite of us in times when we certainly don't deserve it. You may have heard someone say, "Favor isn't fair." However, there are other times when favor comes upon us because of the choices we make. The prophet Daniel is an amazing example of making a choice and God bringing him into a place of favor.

> But Daniel purposed in his heart that he would not defile himself with the portion of the king's meat, nor with the wine which he drank: therefore he requested of the prince of the eunuchs that he might not defile himself. Now God had brought Daniel into favour and tender love with the prince of the eunuchs (Daniel 1:8-9).

Here Daniel did his part and God did His part. One time the Lord said to me, "Adam, I will not do your job and you cannot do Mine." Remember, Daniel made a choice and God brought him into favor. Daniel's stand to be pure caused God to bring him into such favor that a stranger risked his life for Daniel and his friends. Favor is obviously supernatural. Favor is where the natural and the supernatural meet to establish God's will and Kingdom on the earth. Favor is when the supernatural comes into the natural.

Adam LiVecchi ✔ @adamlivecchi
Favor is where the natural and the supernatural meet to establish God's will and Kingdom on the earth.

♡　　⟲　　♡　　✉

The choice that Daniel made also radically benefitted his friends. It's very important to always remember that the decisions we make affect people who are around us and also generations to come. When we live right before God, in purity and in righteousness, it brings other people into their destiny. When our light shines before men, the Father receives glory as people come out of darkness. Later in chapter 2, Daniel makes known to King Nebuchadnezzar the dream he had and the interpretation. Here are the results of that interpretation.

> Then the king made Daniel a great man, and gave him many great gifts, and made him ruler over the whole province of Babylon, and chief of the governors over all the wise men of Babylon. Then Daniel requested of the king, and he set Shadrach, Meshach, and Abednego, over the affairs of the province of Babylon: but Daniel sat in the gate of the king (Daniel 2:48-49).

Daniel's decision to honor God caused his request of the king to be honored. Here Daniel's favor brought his friends into a place of prominence. Not only does your gift make room for you, it makes room for others. Favor is about God entrusting you to reveal who He is to those who can't hear His voice and make room for others. Daniel didn't ask for money or power. He asked for a position for his friends. Here Daniel really reveals the purpose of favor and the heart of the Kingdom. The Kingdom advances through serving others in Jesus' name, so go for it today.

Purpose in your heart to live a life of purity and righteousness. With the sphere of influence God has given you, be sure to make room for others. When someone has the right heart, favor can be very contagious.

Questions

1. Ask the Holy Spirit how you can make room for others today.

    _____

2. Ask the Lord how you can serve others in such a way that it brings those around you into their destiny.

    _____

3. Is there someone specific coming to your mind whom you should have made room for but didn't because of fear or insecurity? If so, ask the Lord Jesus to forgive you and ask Him how to go about dealing with that situation. Also, don't allow satan to try to make you feel guilty of what you may have been unaware of.

    _____

    _____

    _____

    _____

    _____

Prayer of Impartation

Father, help me to steward Your favor with wisdom. Lord, I am asking You to show me how to make room for others. Let my choices open the doors to other people's destiny. Let Your favor rest upon me in such a way that Christ is revealed through my life. Father, we ask all these things in Jesus' name.

Scriptures to Meditate On

And Jesus increased in wisdom and stature, and in favour with God and man (Luke 2:52).

But Daniel purposed in his heart that he would not defile himself with the portion of the king's meat, nor with the wine which he drank: therefore he requested of the prince of the eunuchs that he might not defile himself. Now God had brought Daniel into favour and tender love with the prince of the eunuchs (Daniel 1:8-9).

For thou, Lord, wilt bless the righteous; with favor wilt thou compass him as with a shield (Psalm 5:12).

MATURING IN REVELATION

The more mature a ministry is the more effective it will be in accomplishing that which God has called it to do. Maturity means Holy Spirit-led action that leads to Kingdom advancement. An older, powerful man of God once said to me, "Adam, the Holy Spirit leads, but the devil pushes." The way the Holy Spirit leads is by revelation. The more we mature in revelation, the more we gain wisdom and understanding. Wisdom is the application of revelation to make fruitful that which God has revealed. Understanding is to know the results of the revelation that wisdom was applied correctly. Understanding is to know the outcome before the situation unfolds. Spiritual understanding is supernatural.

Adam LiVecchi ✔ @adamlivecchi
Wisdom is the application of revelation to make fruitful that which God has revealed.

All this is well and good, but first the primary reality is God's love for people and us. If we don't discern the roots or the intentions of God when He gives us revelation, often we won't use it correctly. As I have mentioned before and will mention as long as I have breath in my lungs, Jesus is our example, so let's learn from Him. John 5:19-20 states:

*Then answered Jesus and said unto them, Verily, verily,
I say unto you, The Son can do nothing of himself, but
what he seeth the Father do: for what things soever he
doeth, these also doeth the Son likewise. For the Father
loveth the Son, and sheweth him all things that himself
doeth: and he will show him greater works than these,
that ye may marvel.*

Jesus knew and understood the source of revelation was the Father's love for Him. He knew that the Father loved Him and revealed all things to Him. The word for "love" in the verse above is *phileo*. In Greek it means a benevolent affection. This is the kind of love that grows as you spend time with a person.

This revelation that He received was in the context of ministry. Let me apply this truth to you and me. The Father shows His sons and daughters what they need to do; the real question is, are we paying attention to His Holy Sprit's promptings and leadings? This is not something to feel guilty about if you are not paying attention; it's a fresh invitation to all that God has planned for you in Christ Jesus. If you want to live out His plan, you need to pay attention to His voice and obey what He has said in His Word and is saying by His Holy Spirit. That is what revelation is all about. Revelation is about a love-based cooperation between heaven and earth. The only distance between a believer and their Father in heaven is actually in their own mind. Ephesians 2:6-7 says:

*And hath raised us up together, and made us sit
together in heavenly places in Christ Jesus: that in the
ages to come he might show the exceeding riches of
his grace in his kindness toward us through Christ Jesus.*

The pastor or prophet is not the only one in heavenly places. How can we be seated with Christ in heavenly places yet be right here on planet earth? Good question—the answer is the mind of Christ. We are to be so heavenly minded that we are of earthly good. When our mind is renewed we are useful to ourselves and those around us. When the veil of Jesus' flesh was torn, all separation was eternally gone for those who would believe. That is pretty good news.

The same way the Father revealed things to Jesus and the apostles, He desires to reveal them to us. If His Kingdom is continually increasing in reality, we are not living with an inferior reality, now, are we? I want to show you what maturing in revelation looks like. Matthew 5:3 says, "*Blessed are the poor in spirit: for theirs is the kingdom of heaven.*" Jesus is poor in spirit personified; just hear His total dependency on His Father. John 5:19 states:

> *Then answered Jesus and said unto them, Verily, verily, I say unto you, The Son can do nothing of himself, but what he seeth the Father do: for what things soever he doeth, these also doeth the Son likewise.*

This reality in Jesus' life caused Him to say this to His disciples. John 15:5 states:

> *I am the vine, ye are the branches: He that abideth in me, and I in him, the same bringeth forth much fruit: for without me ye can do nothing.*

To understand this reality means that we are poor in Spirit. Some Christians take twenty years to figure out that they can do nothing without Jesus. My friendly advice is to just believe Jesus when He speaks and you will save yourself so much heartache and pain. We must mature from the place of *we can do nothing without Him* to *we can do all things through Him*. If this truth doesn't become our reality and experience, we will stunt our growth, so to speak. It is God's will for you to grow in revelation and walk in fruitfulness. Therefore, when the Holy Spirit reveals something to you, act on it because often your act of obedience will activate the miraculous. When you act on the revelation that God has given you, someone else will encounter Jesus in a powerful and life-changing way, so go for it today in Jesus' name.

Questions

1. Do you know how to position yourself to receive revelation from God?

   _____

   _____

   _____

2. What revelation have you received from the Lord Jesus lately?

   _____

   _____

   _____

   _____

3. How can you act on that revelation?

   _____

   _____

   _____

   _____

Prayer of Impartation

Father, would You give me a spirit of wisdom and revelation in the knowledge of Your precious Son Jesus. Show Your love for me by revealing Your Son Jesus to me. Let me mature in revelation so that I can do all that You have commanded me. As You give me revelation, let me steward it with wisdom and gain understanding. Let me be fruitful in every good word and increase in the knowledge of God. Father, I ask all these things by Your Holy Spirit in the name of Jesus Christ.

Scriptures to Meditate On

That the God of our Lord Jesus Christ, the Father of glory, may give unto you the spirit of wisdom and revelation in the knowledge of him: The eyes of your understanding being enlightened; that ye may know what is the hope of his calling, and what the riches of the glory of his inheritance in the saints (Ephesians 1:17-18).

And hath raised us up together, and made us sit together in heavenly places in Christ Jesus: that in the ages to come he might show the exceeding riches of his grace in his kindness toward us through Christ Jesus (Ephesians 2:6-7).

I can do all things through Christ which strengtheneth me (Philippians 4:13).

DEMONSTRATION AND EXPLANATION

How the gospel comes is directly connected to who is sent to preach it. There is no such thing as a powerless gospel. If it is powerless, it's not the gospel Jesus or the apostles preached. The gospel is the power of God unto salvation according to the Holy Spirit through the pen of Paul the apostle to the Romans. There is no such thing as a powerless church either. If the gates of hell are prevailing, it's not the church. The gospel comes two ways. It comes through proclamation and demonstration or demonstration and explanation. I will qualify this statement biblically.

> Luke 9:2: *"And he sent them to preach the kingdom of God, and to heal the sick."* (This is proclamation and demonstration.)

> Luke 10:9: *"And heal the sick that are therein, and say unto them, The kingdom of God is come nigh unto you."* (This is demonstration and explanation.)

Please keep in mind that Luke was the only gospel written by and to Gentiles. Therefore, there must be some ways or patterns in that Gospel for reaching the lost. Just a thought.

When Jesus was moving in the office of teacher or rabbi, He demonstrated and then explained the Kingdom of God in Mark 2:1-13. When He was moving in the office of an evangelist, He proclaimed and then demonstrated the Kingdom in Matthew 4:23 and Luke 9:11. Jesus' ministry is the purest look at the five-fold ministry you will ever see. Jesus' model of equipping is similar to the slogan "just do it." He led by example and then created opportunities for His disciples to actually do what He taught them. They, and we, were the beneficiaries of His style of true Kingdom leadership. Matthew 5:19 states:

> Whosoever therefore shall break one of these least
> commandments, and shall teach men so, he shall
> be called the least in the kingdom of heaven: but
> whosoever shall do and teach them, the same shall be
> called great in the kingdom of heaven.

To be great in the Kingdom, first your priorities must be in order. First you do what is right and then you teach others to do what is right. In the Kingdom, the only way to lead is by example. The Kingdom of God is about making disciples, not friends. The Kingdom of God is not a social club with a twist of Jesus. Jesus is not Someone who should just be remembered on Sunday.

Real disciples are made through an authentic gospel. Remember, a fake and watered-down gospel cannot produce real disciples. Now do you see the problem? You have people in churches trying to disciple people who are not even disciples themselves. This creates sustainable hypocrisy. True disciples are only produced through being sent to preach the gospel and demonstrate the Kingdom. Disciples are not made in a Bible study or a house of prayer or even by reading this manual. All those things are good, and I enjoy Bible study and corporate prayer. However, disciples are made in the highways and in the byways. It's not only prayer or study or outreach; it is the combination of all of three. The only kind of evangelism found in the New Testament is where signs and wonders follow those who believe.

If the supernatural element of the gospel is taken out of the gospel, it does not properly represent Jesus. Both His birth and death were completely supernatural. Love is supernatural in a world full of hate. Generosity is supernatural in a world filled with lust and greed. The supernatural part of Christianity is not just about healings and miracles; it is about a life that is supernaturally transformed and radically different. Let me say it like this—many Christians need to get out of bed with the world. Our life is a message whether we are speaking or not. The question is, if someone watched our life would they see Jesus?

There are times when preaching the gospel creates faith because faith comes by hearing. However, there are also times when the demonstration of miracles is necessary to get the attention of unbelievers. This is especially true among the unreached people or among those who have seen phony baloney and/or powerless Christianity. There is a similar concept in the Old Testament. Before God gave Israel a law, He delivered them. The law was to keep them free, not bound. Israel was given the law so that by meditating on it and doing it they would recognize the Christ or Messiah who would come to fulfill it. The law was their schoolmaster to Christ (see Gal. 3:24), meaning that it is to teach us that we need Him and cause us to recognize Him and what He did. God demonstrated His power and gave them a reason to obey His word. He showed them that He had their best interests at heart.

Often when the Kingdom is demonstrated, people really want the King. The power of God illustrates the love of God in ways that people can experience and remember. We are forever indebted to the Lord Jesus Christ for redeeming us. We owe the world an encounter with Jesus, and we owe Jesus the nations because they are His inheritance according to Psalm 2:8. He has merely sent us to collect what He already purchased with His blood on the Cross. Whether you believe it or not, you are a missionary, and you have been ordained and sent to do the work of the Kingdom. The Kingdom comes when the gospel is preached.

That is where you and I come in. Jesus has entrusted us with the good news of His Kingdom. Matthew 13:11 states:

> *He answered and said unto them, Because it is given unto you to know the mysteries of the kingdom of heaven, but to them it is not given.*

Therefore, we must be good stewards of the mysteries we have been entrusted with. According to Matthew 25:14-30, a good steward is one who takes risks on behalf of his master.

Questions

1. Are you willing to take risks for the Kingdom?

   _____

   _____

2. Are you called to preach the gospel? If so, is there anywhere specific that you feel God is leading you?

   _____

   _____

3. According to the New Testament, are miracles normal when the gospel is preached?

   _____

   _____

Prayer of Impartation

Father, in Jesus' name, I thank You that You have called, chosen, ordained, and sent this child of Yours to preach and demonstrate the Kingdom of God. I pray that I would be willing to take risks. I pray that I would not follow signs and wonders but that signs and wonders would follow me as I follow You. From the place of intimacy let authentic Kingdom ministry flow. Holy Spirit, lead me to the specific places and specific people so the Father will be glorified as I obey Your Son Jesus.

GO. PREACH. HEAL.

Scriptures to Meditate On

For whosoever shall call upon the name of the Lord shall be saved. How then shall they call on him in whom they have not believed? and how shall they believe in him of whom they have not heard? and how shall they hear without a preacher? and how shall they preach, except they be sent? as it is written, How beautiful are the feet of them that preach the gospel of peace, and bring glad tidings of good things! (Romans 10:13-15)

And he sent them to preach the kingdom of God, and to heal the sick (Luke 9:2).

And heal the sick that are therein, and say unto them, The kingdom of God is come nigh unto you (Luke 10:9).

INTENTIONAL.
STRATEGIC. SUPERNATURAL.

The ministry of the Lord Jesus Christ was intentional, strategic, and supernatural. You are called to continue His ministry. Those who continue in His word are His disciples because continuing in His word causes us to continue in His work. The word and the work should be synonymous. When the word is declared, the Holy Spirit moves; this is ministry. As you mature in the ministry God has called you to, your ministry will be just like His because Jesus will be living His life through you. Ministry is the life of God flowing through human beings in Jesus' name.

Luke 14:28 states, *"For which of you, intending to build a tower, sitteth not down first, and counteth the cost, whether he have sufficient to finish it?"* In the Kingdom we must be intentional about what we are building. When we count the cost, we must be intentional and strategic in terms of where and with whom we are building. Sometimes people can build the right things with the wrong people and that certainly will not pay off in the end. In the Kingdom, relationships are crucial. Also, nothing in the Kingdom is built naturally. Everything God does is supernatural. It is natural to Him but supernatural to us. God is naturally supernatural and through Christ in us we become naturally supernatural because we are partakers of the divine nature.

> *After these things the Lord appointed other seventy also, and sent them two and two before his face into*

*every city and place, whither he himself would come.
Therefore said he unto them, The harvest truly is great,
but the labourers are few: pray ye therefore the Lord
of the harvest, that he would send forth labourers into
his harvest. Go your ways: behold, I send you forth as
lambs among wolves* (Luke 10:1-3).

Here we see the strategic, the intentional, and the supernatural all working together. Let me say it like this—the will of God is strategic, intentional, and supernatural. When Jesus said the harvest is plentiful but the laborers are few, He was saying that the problem is not in the building but outside the building. It is not that God doesn't want to save or that people don't want to get saved but that people don't want to go and preach and demonstrate the Kingdom. Here Jesus discerns the nature of the issue and the conditions of the hearts of His people. Being intentional and strategic begins with discernment. Then that discernment gets expressed through the knowledge of what is discerned. Then it gets applied through wisdom.

Understanding often causes one to know the results before wisdom is applied. Jesus knew the problem was the lack of laborers for the plentiful harvest, so He, being intentional, caused His disciples to be the solution to the problem. He, being strategic, sent His disciples to places He Himself would later show up. God still is strategic, and He sends us to places He Himself intends to show up. When God sends a believer, He has predetermined to manifest His presence. When a believer shows up, Christ shows up because He lives in believers and fully intends to live His life and manifest His presence through them.

This is completely supernatural. Jesus sent the disciples to heal the sick and cast out devils—He commanded them to be supernatural. When we obey Jesus, we become supernatural. There is no way you can obey Jesus according to the Scriptures and not be supernatural. Without Jesus we can do nothing, but through Him we can do all things because He strengthens us. Now is a time of action and demonstration; now is the time to do something with what we have received from God. The key to receiving in the Kingdom is giving. Being faithful is both intentional and strategic. Faithfulness causes supernatural growth and spiritual acceleration.

God is eternal and all-knowing; therefore, everything He does is intentional. The more we mature spiritually, the more intentional and strategic we become. Being Holy Spirit-led is about being intentional, strategic, and supernatural. If you want to see what it looks like to be led by the Holy Spirit, just look at Jesus—He is our perfect example in all things. If you can't show it to me with Jesus, I am just not interested. Jesus is our living, walking, and talking manual. He came to show us the Father, and when our light shines before men the Father receives glory. The Son of God and the sons of the Kingdom are sent to do the works of the Father that He might be revealed. John 15:15 states:

> Henceforth I call you not servants; for the servant
> knoweth not what his lord doeth: but I have called you
> friends; for all things that I have heard of my Father I
> have made known unto you.

Revelation changes our identity and makes us strategic. If we want to partner with God in the earth, we need to know what He is doing. As believers who hear God's voice and follow Him, we should know where He is leading us. If we don't, it is not God's fault; it is actually our problem. The issue is not "Is God speaking?" The real issue is "Are we listening?" First Timothy 4:1 says:

> Now the Spirit speaketh expressly, that in the latter
> times some shall depart from the faith, giving heed to
> seducing spirits, and doctrines of devils.

I realize that this verse is speaking about the last days. However, there is a principle about the ministry of the Holy Spirit we need for right now.

When it says the Spirit speaketh *expressly*, it actually means *distinctly*. God can communicate in such a way that you will clearly understand that which He communicates. If we can communicate clearly with God, we can be intentional, strategic, and supernatural. To finish the ministry of Jesus, we will need to be all three.

> **Adam LiVecchi** ✔ @adamlivecchi
> If we can communicate clearly with God, we can be intentional, strategic, and supernatural.

Love should always be our motive because love is powerful and doesn't lack anything needed to fulfill its mission. When the Father gave Jesus, it was love in motion. Love is intentional, strategic, and supernatural. Love is not ignorant or clueless to that which God is doing. Love increases in both knowledge and discernment. Philippians 1:9 states, "*And this I pray, that your love may abound yet more and more in knowledge and in all judgment.*" The word for "judgment" here actually means *discernment*. We increase in knowledge and in discernment so we can be more effective in the ministry and come to know Jesus more intimately.

As we do the work of the ministry, we increase in the knowledge of God. Working with God causes us to know God. When we really know God, we are His friends and we clearly know and discern what He is doing. When we enter into friendship with God, the mystery of God's will turns into the knowledge of His will. Revelation is the unveiling of the unseen. When God releases revelation, it is to change who we are and how we think and live. Increasing in wisdom and spiritual understanding also allows us to be intentional, strategic, and supernatural. God's will should not remain a mystery to you your whole life, because if it does you might not do anything with Jesus or for people. A lot of people live like they don't know what God said in His word; this causes them to not be led by the Holy Spirit because of unbelief. False humility is often manifested because of unbelief. Often false humility says, "I don't know what God is doing." If you are His friend, then you should know what He is doing.

Knowing what God is doing is a privilege, and it also releases a responsibility. To aid in this, the solution is read your Bible and practice what it clearly teaches us to do. Knowing what He has said will help you know what He can and will do. Revelation changes our identity and friendship causes us to see our assignment. In Genesis 18:17 and Exodus 32:10-11, there are several examples of friendship with God. In both of these examples, relationship or friendship with God releases a responsibility to the one who is His friend. Others should always benefit from our relationship with God. Through friendship with God we become intentional, strategic, and supernatural.

Questions

1. Can you find another example of a Bible character being strategic, intentional, and supernatural?

    _____

    _____

    _____

2. What was the result of that person being strategic, intentional, and supernatural?

    _____

    _____

    _____

3. Ask the Lord how you can be strategic, intentional, and supernatural.

    _____

    _____

    _____

Prayer of Impartation

Father, I pray that I would increase in love and discernment. Let me be filled with wisdom, knowledge, and understanding. Cause me to be intentional, strategic, and supernatural. Let me increase in the knowledge of God as I partner with You. I pray these things in Jesus' name.

Scriptures to Meditate On

After these things the Lord appointed other seventy also, and sent them two and two before his face into every city and place, whither he himself would come. Therefore said he unto them, The harvest truly is great, but the labourers are few: pray ye therefore the Lord of the harvest, that he would send forth labourers into his harvest. Go your ways: behold, I send you forth as lambs among wolves (Luke 10:1-3).

Henceforth I call you not servants; for the servant knoweth not what his lord doeth: but I have called you friends; for all things that I have heard of my Father I have made known unto you (John 15:15).

And this I pray, that your love may abound yet more and more in knowledge and in all judgment (Philippians 1:9).

THE GREAT COMMANDMENT AND THE GREAT COMMISSION

The key to giving love away is to first receive it from God so His love can flow through us. The great commandment is the fuel for the great commission. Some people think the great commission is fuel for the great commandment, yet this is not true. Jesus first commanded His disciples to love God and one another; then He commanded them to go into all the world and preach to everyone everywhere. The first commandment to love God with all that you are is expressed in loving people. When we separate our love for God and our love for people, we have actually left our first love. According to Jesus and Paul love is an action. John 3:16 and First Thessalonians 1:3 talk about love as an action. In First Corinthians 13, we see what love does and what loves does not do. Revelation 2:4-5 states:

> *Nevertheless I have somewhat against thee, because thou hast left thy first love. Remember therefore from whence thou art fallen, and repent, and do the first works; or else I will come unto thee quickly, and will remove thy candlestick out of his place, except thou repent.*

Here we see that the church in Ephesus (modern-day Turkey) left its first love, which caused them to not do their first works. The first love/

first works connection is biblically inseparable. The question is what were their first works? Great question! In Acts 19:1-12, we see it was *power evangelism*. Here Paul the apostle trained twelve men and they reached everyone in the city with the gospel.

> **Adam LiVecchi** ● @adamlivecchi
> Our privilege is to know God; our responsibility is to make Him known.

The gospel Paul preached was demonstrated with "special" miracles. There was an irrefutable witness of unforgettable power demonstrating the real Jesus. This is what creation is groaning for. All of creation is groaning for us to become like the Jesus who lives on the inside of us. Creation desires sons to manifest the Son. Maturity means we manifest Christ to those who need Him; this involves wisdom, power, and godly character. Paul argued for three months but he also demonstrated the Kingdom in such a way that all arguments ceased. In fulfilling the great commission, we will have to be able to defend our faith and demonstrate our faith. Standing up for our faith is defensive and demonstrating it is offensive, and to win we will need to do both. We defend our faith by our reactions; we demonstrate our faith by our actions. Both defending and demonstrating our faith is crucial when it comes to bringing people to Jesus. Bill Johnson said, "We owe the world an encounter with Jesus." When the Kingdom comes, a decision must be made. Steve Stewart said, "When the Kingdom comes everything changes." People will have to choose to accept Jesus or reject Him. When the Kingdom is manifested, the King is revealed. Our privilege is to know God; our responsibility is to make Him known.

When you love people you don't want them to be sick, under demonic oppression, and you certainly don't want them to go to hell. Therefore, the great commission becomes an expression of your love for God and people. When we value what Jesus did on the cross, we will bring Him the reward of His suffering. Jesus is the desire of the nations, and they are His inheritance. We live in the gap between Him and them. Our mission is to invite them to a wedding feast so that the Father's house will be full. My spiritual father, Steve Stewart, once told me, "The church doesn't have a mission; the mission has a church." The great commission has two primary expressions. They are as follows:

> And Jesus came and spake unto them, saying, All power is given unto me in heaven and in earth. Go ye therefore, and teach all nations, baptizing them in the name of the Father, and of the Son, and of the Holy Ghost: teaching them to observe all things whatsoever I have commanded you: and, lo, I am with you always, even unto the end of the world. Amen (Matthew 28:18-20).

> And he said unto them, Go ye into all the world, and preach the gospel to every creature. He that believeth and is baptized shall be saved; but he that believeth not shall be damned. And these signs shall follow them that believe; In my name shall they cast out devils; they shall speak with new tongues; they shall take up serpents; and if they drink any deadly thing, it shall not hurt them; they shall lay hands on the sick, and they shall recover (Mark 16:15-18).

In the Gospel of Matthew, we are focused on teaching nations or people to obey all things that Jesus commanded. In Mark we are commanded to preach the gospel to everyone everywhere. Matthew is clearly focusing on discipleship and Mark is clearly focused on evangelism. It is not one or the other; it is both. To put it simply, often people miss God's will when they deviate from His plan or mission. Often God's will and our agenda just don't work together, so we must choose. To find God's will, we must surrender ours. Either Jesus is Lord and we obey Him or we become god unto ourselves by doing whatever we want, whenever we want. The key to total misery is just to do whatever we want and then go to church on Sunday. One of the keys to joy is to do those things that are pleasing to God, and we will feel or experience His pleasure through our choices that honor Him. When the disciples were sent out in Luke 10, they returned with joy. When we love Jesus and serve others we become filled with joy as we take our eyes off of ourselves and put them on Jesus and those whom He has paid for with His very own blood.

Jesus commanded His disciples to go into all the world and preach to every creature because He was not willing that any should perish; therefore, He tasted death for every man. We can taste and see that He is good because He tasted death for every man. The great commission is just simply bringing Jesus what already belongs to Him anyway. This is your job should you choose to say yes. The good news is that a generation of people will say yes, and the job will get done. Jesus will receive the reward of His suffering. Honestly, I believe you are the people and the time is now. To further stir your faith for harvest, let's look briefly at the book of Revelation.

> And I beheld, and, lo, in the midst of the throne and of
> the four beasts, and in the midst of the elders, stood
> a Lamb as it had been slain, having seven horns and
> seven eyes, which are the seven Spirits of God sent
> forth into all the earth. And he came and took the book
> out of the right hand of him that sat upon the throne.
> And when he had taken the book, the four beasts and
> four and twenty elders fell down before the Lamb,
> having every one of them harps, and golden vials full of

odours, which are the prayers of saints. And they sung
a new song, saying, Thou art worthy to take the book,
and to open the seals thereof: for thou wast slain, and
hast redeemed us to God by thy blood out of every
kindred, and tongue, and people, and nation; and hast
made us unto our God kings and priests: and we shall
reign on the earth (Revelation 5:6-10).

The seven spirits of God are sent forth into all the earth because the church is sent forth into all the earth. One of the end results of the Holy Spirit being sent into all the earth is people being redeemed from every tribe, tongue, kindred, and nation. There will be a generation fully gripped by the sacrifice of Jesus Christ. When Jesus said, "It is finished," He meant it. That is amazing, but there is even more. Revelation 11:15 states:

And the seventh angel sounded; and there were great
voices in heaven, saying, The kingdoms of this world
are become the kingdoms of our Lord, and of his Christ;
and he shall reign for ever and ever.

That is amazing, but there is even more. Revelation 21:1-4 states:

And I saw a new heaven and a new earth: for the first
heaven and the first earth were passed away; and there
was no more sea. And I John saw the holy city, new
Jerusalem, coming down from God out of heaven,
prepared as a bride adorned for her husband. And I
heard a great voice out of heaven saying, Behold, the
tabernacle of God is with men, and he will dwell with
them, and they shall be his people, and God himself
shall be with them, and be their God. And God shall
wipe away all tears from their eyes; and there shall

be no more death, neither sorrow, nor crying, neither shall there be any more pain: for the former things are passed away.

This is really good news. When the blood of Jesus dripped on this planet, He paid for all things to be made new. God is doing so many amazing things in the earth in our day.

Questions

These questions are asked twice for a reason.

1. Will you go?

_____

_____

_____

2. Where is God saying to go?

_____

_____

_____

3. When will you go?

_____

_____

_____

Prayer of Impartation

Father, let the fire of Your Son's sacrifice burn on the altar of my heart. Cause me to walk in the revelation of Jesus' sacrifice. Let me be fully gripped by the gospel of the Kingdom. Let me be a partaker of the power of the age to come as they labor in Your harvest. May I never look back. I pray these things in Jesus' name.

Scriptures to Meditate On

Ask of me, and I shall give thee the heathen for thine inheritance, and the uttermost parts of the earth for thy possession (Psalm 2:8).

All the ends of the world shall remember and turn unto the Lord: and all the kindreds of the nations shall worship before thee. For the kingdom is the Lord's: and he is the governor among the nations (Psalm 22:27-28).

The Lord said unto my Lord, Sit thou at my right hand, until I make thine enemies thy footstool (Psalm 110:1).

PRACTICAL. TACTICAL. SUPERNATURAL.

In this section of the manual we are going to touch on the practical, the tactical, and the supernatural aspects of ministry. We must go from just doing outreaches to becoming an outreach. We don't need more programs. We need to get on board with the Kingdom that is ever increasing. As we mature in doing outreaches consistently, we actually create a lifestyle and a culture of reaching out. In the Kingdom there is one direction and that is forward. The next section will give you some practical and supernatural ways of going forward in ministry.

Adam LiVecchi ✔ @adamlivecchi
Warning: Proceed with caution. If you put the truth into action, it may cause some problems!

♡   ↻   ♡   ✉

Practical tips for spending time with God in the secret place:

1. Go to a place where you can be quiet and uninterrupted by people or distractions. The most important time of your life is the time you spend alone with God and

completely focused on Him. Some people call it seeking God. I don't call it this because He is not lost and neither are you if you are a Christian. Instead of seeking a God who found us when we were not looking for Him, we need to focus on Him and have uninterrupted communion with Him. This needs to be daily and consistent.

2. Go to a place where you can be alone.

3. Shut off your phone and the e-mail program on your computer.

4. Take a journal with you, whether it is pen and paper or a journal on your computer, laptop, netbook, or iPad. When you have something to write with you are actually preparing to hear from God. Remember, it is way more important what He can say to you than what you can say to Him. He already knows everything you are going to say. So go into the secret place with the posture of listening first. The Father tells secrets in the secret place, so listen.

JOURNALING

Journaling is one of the most important habits you will develop. Where your Bible is, there your journal should be also. If we really value what God says we will write it down. The key to receiving more is to be faithful with what you have. Before I ever wrote a book I had about eight to ten journals filled up with what I was doing, what God was saying, and what God was doing. Pouring your heart out on paper to God is a worthwhile investment.

> **Adam LiVecchi** ✔ @adamlivecchi
> The key to receiving more is to be faithful with what you have.
>
> 💬   🔁   🤍   ✉

On a more practical side, if I were you I wouldn't buy a cheap journal. If I were you I would buy a nice journal that you will want to write in and save. What God says and does is priceless. Ten or fifteen dollars is a small price to pay to have what God said to you in a nice organized book that will last you. There are some people who would just buy a cheap notebook; the chances of them having their journals in twenty-five years are less than likely. The chances of me having my journals in twenty-five years are certain as long as the creek doesn't rise.

I wonder if all the people who wrote the Hebrew Scriptures and the Greek New Testament knew their writing would make what we call the Holy Scriptures. When I say Holy Scriptures, I mean the inspired and infallible the Word of God. Second Timothy 3:16 states, "*All scripture is given by inspiration of God, and is profitable for doctrine, for reproof, for correction, for instruction in righteousness.*" I am not suggesting that my writing or your writing is equal to Scripture—that would be heretical. What I am simply stating again is that those who value what God says and does will write it down.

Practically speaking, journaling is part of the legacy you will leave to your children. Often when people think of inheritance all they think of is money, but in reality an inheritance is more than dollars and cents. According to the Scriptures, what God reveals belongs to you and your children. Deuteronomy 29:29 states, "*The secret things belong unto the Lord our God: but those things which are revealed belong unto us and to our children for ever, that we may do all the words of this law.*" If something belongs to you and your children, perhaps you may want to have it on file. (Okay, I am going to stop trying to convince you to buy a journal.)

Here is a practical example of journaling:

- Date: month/day/year

- Place: where you are as you journal

- Fasting: If you are fasting, include that at the top of your journal entry. Include what kind of fast.

- Communion: If you take communion by yourself or at your house, write down what is going on in your heart before taking communion. I suggest you take communion by yourself at home, if you don't already. You don't need to wait for a pastor or leader to give you a piece of bread.

What to Journal About?

- Write briefly the highlights and/or the low points of your day.

- If you want to make confession about sin, writing it down may help. If you felt the Holy Spirit leading you to confess your sin to a natural person, make sure it is someone you can trust.

- Whenever God does something supernatural in your life, write it down.

- Write down your prayers so when God answers them you can have evidence that God is involved in your life. This, in my opinion, will really strengthen your faith, especially when you go back and look at what God has done.

- Most believers don't really know how to pour out their soul to God. Learning to do this is of the upmost value. Here is a good example. First Samuel 1:15 states, *"And Hannah answered and said, No, my lord, I am a woman of a sorrowful spirit: I have drunk neither wine nor strong drink, but have poured out my soul before the Lord."* One of the keys to a clear conscience and a healthy soul life is to pour out your soul to God. Reading the word of God daily, confessing sin, and praying in tongues are some others.

- Write down dreams, visions, and prophecy. Test the spirit and the word to see whether they are of God.

- Write down questions you may have about the circumstances in your life.

- Write down any insight you get about current events. Another thing—if you look back into your old journal entries God just may give you new insight.

As you write these things down, you will need a code so that when you go back to look at what God has said and done you can do it in an orderly and timely fashion.

You can use the left-hand side of the page for the abbreviations. Circle the letter abbreviations to make it easy for you to find what you are looking for. The more disciplined your journaling is, the more fruitful your journaling will be over time.

(Keep in mind these are just examples to help jump-start your journaling habits. Also they are not in any specific order of priority.)

T: test, trial, or even tribulation

P: divine protection

H: healing

S: when you lead someone to Jesus

G: when God tells you to give something that seems to be out of the ordinary. It could be money or a material thing but is not limited to that.

Pr: when you receive something prophetic from God or a person

V: when you get a victory in your private life

J: when you do justice. Remember one of the expressions of love is justice.

$: when you receive a financial breakthrough or miraculous provision

FIVE-STEP HEALING MODEL

This five-step healing model has been used by John Wimber, Randy Clark, Steve Stewart, and many others in the body of Christ. It is practical. It's not a rule; it's a tool. It will give you a grid to pray for the sick whether they are on the street or at the altar in church. It gives you a context to pray for an absolute stranger. If you know the person or what is wrong with the person you can skip a few steps.

1. Introduction: Hi, my name is _____ ; you are?

2. Diagnostic: Find out what is wrong with the person. The condition may be visible, but it may not be.

3. Invite the Holy Spirit: Listen to God and gently lay your hands on the person.

4. Command the healing in Jesus' name!

5. Test it out: Have the person do something they couldn't do before you prayed.

Introduction

Be polite and smile. God is in a good mood and you should be too. If this part doesn't go well you may never get to steps two to five.

Diagnostic

Be sensitive and compassionate; the condition may have been tormenting the person for quite some time. Often people who are afflicted for a long time are touchy because of the pain. Don't make assumptions, just ask questions.

Invite the Holy Spirit

You may even say, "Jesus, let (person receiving prayer) experience Your love right now." Always ask for permission before you lay hands on someone. Always be gentle. (The "Pentecostal push" is a real turn off.) If it is someone of the opposite sex, always put your hands in an appropriate place. When praying for someone of the opposite sex, allow enough room between you and the person for other people to see that your hands are in an honorable place. All through the process, listen to God. If you get an impression in your mind, ask the person about the impression you are getting. Don't tell them "thus saith the Lord." If it *is* a "thus saith the Lord," you won't have to say any of that stuff. Often you may get a word of knowledge about someone's past or present or a prophetic word about his or her future. This really builds faith, so remember to listen to God. If your impression is asked in question form you can say "I am sorry about that" and proceed to command healing. (This is a very brief example; I will share more details later on moving in the prophetic.)

Command

Command the healing in Jesus' name! We are not asking God to heal the sick. He commanded us to in Matthew 10:7-8. The stripes on

Jesus' back show us God's will. We are speaking to the condition with the authority Jesus gave us.

Now here is a free lesson I learned in Mexico. When you command healing and the pain moves, it's a demon. Instead of commanding healing, you need to command the spirit of infirmity to leave the person's body. Again, we are not asking the demon to leave; we are commanding him to leave in Jesus' name. Don't pray a long prayer. Always keep your eyes opened. Keeping your eyes opened can allow you to see the spirit move on someone or protect you from any sudden movements from the person you're praying for. Nowhere in the Bible does it say to close your eyes when you pray.

Adam LiVecchi ✔ @adamlivecchi
"Not everyone gets healed, but everyone must get loved!" —Randy Clark

Test It Out

Don't force anyone to do anything. You can tell them to test it out, but if they say no, proceed in a gentle way. It's the obedience of faith that activates the miraculous. Be alert and cautious. If someone couldn't walk and now they have faith to walk, be ready to jump up and down and celebrate with them or catch them. Having someone fall would really work in a negative way. Don't be afraid, but be cautious. The dignity of other people is a huge deal. Randy Clark said this and I love it: "Not everyone gets healed, but everyone must get loved!" The most important part of this whole process is that we communicate the love of God to them in all that we say and do. If your hands don't heal people, your shadow never will, so step out in faith and see God move in power.

Questions

1. Is healing for today, or did God change His mind?

   _____

   _____

   _____

   _____

2. Biblically speaking, are you called to heal the sick?

   _____

   _____

   _____

   _____

3. Do you have to accept Jesus as your Savior for Him to heal you?

   _____

   _____

   _____

   _____

Prayer of Impartation

Father, in Jesus' name would You continually reveal to me the price that Jesus paid for people to be healed. Holy Spirit, would You release the gift of healing, the gift of faith, and the working of miracles. May I function in detailed words of knowledge especially when I am ministering healing. Let the prophetic be in full operation as I minister healing and deliverance. Cause me to move with the discerning of spirits when they are ministering to the sick. Use me powerfully to advance Your Kingdom through the ministry of healing. Let people be born again continually as I minster healing to the sick and the lost. I pray these things in Jesus' name.

Healing Scriptures to Meditate On

Who forgiveth all thine iniquities; who healeth all thy diseases (Psalm 103:3).

But he was wounded for our transgressions, he was bruised for our iniquities: the chastisement of our peace was upon him; and with his stripes we are healed (Isaiah 53:5).

Whether is it easier to say to the sick of the palsy, Thy sins be forgiven thee; or to say, Arise, and take up thy bed, and walk? But that ye may know that the Son of man hath power on earth to forgive sins, (he saith to the sick of the palsy,) I say unto thee, Arise, and take up thy bed, and go thy way into thine house. And immediately he arose, took up the bed, and went forth before them all; insomuch that they were all amazed, and glorified God, saying, We never saw it on this fashion (Mark 2:9-12).

How God anointed Jesus of Nazareth with the Holy Ghost and with power: who went about doing good, and healing all that were oppressed of the devil; for God was with him (Acts 10:38).

And the very God of peace sanctify you wholly; and I pray God your whole spirit and soul and body be preserved blameless unto the coming of our Lord Jesus Christ (1 Thessalonians 5:23).

And he shewed me a pure river of water of life, clear as crystal, proceeding out of the throne of God and of the Lamb. In the midst of the street of it, and on either side of the river, was there the tree of life, which bare twelve manner of fruits, and yielded her fruit every month: and the leaves of the tree were for the healing of the nations (Revelation 22:1-2).

Your Healing Testimonies

Below are some lines for you to fill with healing testimonies. Remember, physical healings are actually lives rescued from the grip of the enemy.

DELIVERANCE

Jesus cast out demons, and He commanded us to do the same; therefore, we must. Jesus said it and that settles it. His word is forever settled in heaven; now it needs to be settled in our hearts and heads as well. When God's word is settled in our hearts and in our heads, it will be manifested and established in our lives. You may hear someone say, "Healing and deliverance are not for today." Someone who says that may have some unbelief they need to be vaccinated of. It is not only unbelief; it is also deception. Unbelief always leads to deception. To say that Jesus Christ is the same yesterday, today, and forever and not believe that He still does today what He did through weak people in the Gospels and in the book of Acts is to deny who Jesus really is. It is an insult to the blood of Jesus to say that He doesn't heal or deliver people from demons today. Unbelief is a sin against God. In my opinion, it is one of the greatest if not the greatest manifestations of wickedness in the church today.

Mark 16:17 states, *"And these signs shall follow them that believe; In my name shall they cast out devils; they shall speak with new tongues."* Here deliverance is classified as a sign. A sign points to a greater truth. Satan was cast down from heaven to the earth. When he came to earth after the fall of man, he then fed on the dust of the earth. Man came from the dust of the earth; therefore, mankind literally became the devil's lunch. However, there was a prophecy about a seed who would bruise the serpent's head and the serpent would bruise His heel. This prophecy was made manifest when Jesus' feet were nailed to the tree. Jesus' feet were bruised and the serpent's head was crushed.

The cross and the resurrection manifested the victory prophesied about in Genesis 3:15. Jesus, who is the Word of God, cast the devil out of heaven and down to the earth. He also came to the earth casting demons out of people. The demons in people knew who Jesus was, perhaps because they knew the authority of His voice. Jesus didn't just cast out demons; He also commanded us to do that very same thing. When a demon or demons are cast out of a person, it is a sign that points to the day the devil and all his minions will be thrown off the earth forever into the lake of fire. Perhaps now you see why satan doesn't like deliverance? Revelation 20:10 states, *"And the devil that deceived them was cast into the lake of fire and brimstone, where the beast and the false prophet are, and shall be tormented day and night for ever and ever."* Until this happens, it is our job to cast demons out of people and displace satan's authority by extending the Kingdom of God.

I will share a testimony with you from Haiti. It was April of 2010, just several months after the nation-shaking earthquake that took over 230,000 lives. My whole family went to Haiti with me, and it was an unforgettable mission trip. I was so grateful to be on a trip with my whole family. We all stayed in tents at a pastor's house in Carrefour, Haiti. One afternoon, a young man who was possessed with demons grabbed a handful of rocks and began to swallow them. Immediately, some of the Haitian men, my brother, and I jumped on him, pinned him down, and began to pull the rocks out of his mouth. Truly, the enemy comes to steal, kill, and destroy. By the grace of God we were able to get all of the rocks out his mouth before he could swallow any of them.

There was a group of us standing around. In the group there was an unsaved man observing the demonic activity. The demons were actually speaking through the young man, who was a professing Christian. This may challenge your theology or doctrine, but it is a true story nevertheless. The unsaved man's arms were crossed as he watched, probably not knowing what to think. The demon-possessed young man slapped the unsaved man in the leg and said, "Get saved today or come to hell with me."

At that moment I turned to the man and pointed at him and said, "Today is the day of salvation." Immediately, he dropped to his knees, repented of his sins, and accepted Jesus as his Lord and Savior. Every time I think of this story I marvel at the goodness and the wisdom of God. God can literally use the devil to advance His Kingdom. I will not and am not making any new doctrine; all I am really saying is that God is really in charge.

Here is one more brief testimony. If my memory serves me correctly, it was 2005. I was in a prayer meeting in a church in Nanticoke, Pennsylvania. There was a girl who was not feeling well. She was laid out on a church pew toward the left side of the sanctuary. I felt the Holy Spirit tell me to go blow my shofar right in her face. So I did as I was instructed. As soon as I blew the shofar (or ram's horn), the girl started to manifest demons and throw up. She was delivered from demons not through the blowing of a shofar or because I am anointed, but she was delivered because of obedient faith. Real faith is obedient to what God is saying in the present moment. It is the obedience of faith that activates the miraculous and manifests the power and the authority of God. The Kingdom comes when we obey what the King is saying.

Hearing God is always essential for ministry, especially when it comes to the ministry of deliverance. In the same way the Holy Spirit speaks to the soul of man, so does the demonic. Casting out demons can be different almost every time because people are different and the demonic also deals with the soul realm.

Some Practical Tips When Doing Deliverance

When casting out the devil there should be **one main person** leading the charge. Having people intercede is okay. Jesus didn't need intercessors and neither did the apostles, but it is not at all a bad idea to have other people praying as well.

Remember, we are not asking the demon or demons to leave, we are **commanding them to leave** in Jesus name.

Remember to **listen to the Holy Spirit** when ministering to the demonized. He will give you instructions. If His instructions come through someone else, be humble and open to receive from a brother or sister even if you are the one leading the charge.

The gift of **discerning of sprits** will function while you are casting out demons. If the Holy Spirit tells you the name of the evil spirit, use it when commanding it to go. If you don't get the name of the demon or demons, just proceed to use the authority Jesus gave you in His name.

What is interesting is that a lot of the practices of modern-day deliverance ministry are nowhere to be found in the ministry of Jesus or the apostles. You may hear people say you don't need to raise your voice when speaking to a demon or demons in a person. Yes, that may be true, but the Bible doesn't say not to either. Just allow the Holy Spirit to lead you, because where the Spirit of the Lord is there is freedom. He will lead you perfectly when it comes to getting people the freedom Jesus paid so much for. Remember, deliverance is a *rescued life*, not just a cool testimony.

In deliverance, you're dealing with the devil and someone's free will. Unfortunately there will be times when people will want to hold on to the demon or the devil in them. The sober reality is that **the person has a free will and God will honor it**. According to Matthew 17:21, there are some demons that only come out with prayer and fasting. In this verse I believe Jesus is talking about a lifestyle of prayer and fasting rather than a one-time prayer or fast to get rid of a demon.

Jesus Himself **did not look for the root causes** of how or why a demon took residence in a person; He just cast them out. I am not against identifying the root causes; it's just that Jesus never looked for them. Some root causes can be sin, sexual immorality, lust, rape, abuse, witchcraft, and voodoo. These are only a few.

(Just to make it clear, this is by no means the law on deliverance. The best way to learn how to respond is by experience.)

Questions

1. Can you pray deliverance for yourself?

    _____

2. Are you afraid to cast the devil out of someone?

    _____

3. After you cast out a demon, can you command it where to go?

    _____

Prayer of Impartation

Father, in Jesus' name, would You use me to extend Your Kingdom through the ministry of deliverance. Let the gift of discerning of spirits operate as I minister to the oppressed and the possessed. Let many be set free and healed through my deliverance ministry. Lord, let Your Kingdom come as I pray and prophesy. Give me the love, compassion, wisdom, and perseverance needed to see the oppressed go free. I ask these things in the name of Jesus Christ.

GO. PREACH. HEAL.

Scriptures to Meditate On

The Lord is my rock, and my fortress, and my deliverer; my God, my strength, in whom I will trust; my buckler, and the horn of my salvation, and my high tower (Psalm 18:2).

He brought me forth also into a large place; he delivered me, because he delighted in me (Psalm 18:19).

I sought the Lord, and he heard me, and delivered me from all my fears (Psalm 34:4).

But if I with the finger of God cast out devils, no doubt the kingdom of God is come upon you (Luke 11:20).

THE SIMPLICITY OF THE GOSPEL

The gospel is good news. Some preachers need to tell their faces that! When the message we preach ceases to be good news, it's not the gospel. It is the kindness of God that leads to repentance. Romans 2:4 states, "*Or do you despise the riches of His goodness, forbearance, and longsuffering, not knowing that the goodness of God leads you to repentance?*" (NKJV). Let's see this truth in action.

> And saw two ships standing by the lake: but the
> fishermen were gone out of them, and were washing
> their nets. And he entered into one of the ships, which
> was Simon's, and prayed him that he would thrust out
> a little from the land. And he sat down, and taught the
> people out of the ship. Now when he had left speaking,
> he said unto Simon, Launch out into the deep, and let
> down your nets for a draught. And Simon answering
> said unto him, Master, we have toiled all the night,
> and have taken nothing: nevertheless at thy word I will
> let down the net. And when they had this done, they
> inclosed a great multitude of fishes: and their net brake.
> And they beckoned unto their partners, which were in
> the other ship, that they should come and help them.
> And they came, and filled both the ships, so that they
> began to sink. When Simon Peter saw it, he fell down at
> Jesus' knees, saying, Depart from me; for I am a sinful
> man, O Lord. For he was astonished, and all that were

with him, at the draught of the fishes which they had taken (Luke 5:2-9).

Jesus never mentioned a word about Peter's sin, yet he wound up on his knees acknowledging his sin. The goodness or kindness of God truly does lead to repentance. Peter went from an innocent, hardworking fisherman who fished all night and caught nothing to a guilty fisherman on his knees in front of his employees. The goodness of God is pretty serious business. This probably was the biggest catch of Peter's life, yet all he could see was his sin. It would be like someone winning the Grammys and getting on their knees on TV and asking God to forgive them. God's grace and goodness has a way of making us see our true condition. God's mercy and grace also has a way of totally transforming us if we give ourselves to the process.

Here is the gospel in a nutshell. Everyone everywhere has sinned; we are all guilty. Jesus was not willing that any should perish. Therefore, He tasted death for every man. He died for us while we were still sinning. He didn't wait until we said we were sorry. He said, "Father, forgive them for they know not what they do." That is good news. Jesus was completely aware of our blindness and our arrogant ignorance. But He simply could not live without us. His Father's love for us was so great that Jesus went. He came and put on flesh. He was stripped, whipped, beaten, and pierced. His heart ruptured and His blood was poured out. Then He offered His Spirit up. He did all this for us so that we would have eternal life in Him.

Those who can't receive the good news are in some serious trouble. The good news, when rejected, turns into very bad news. Those who don't believe and won't receive, acknowledge, and obey Jesus will burn in hell forever. God will not send them an apology letter, because Jesus was enough. Take Him or leave Him. It is your choice. He has already chosen you; that is why He sent Jesus. Even our faith in Jesus isn't our own work. God puts His grace toward us so we can put our faith in Him, which is salvation. We are saved from our sins, other people's opinions, the devil, eternal flames, and ourselves. That is some really good news. We can be free from everything, which makes us free to obey all that Jesus commanded. The gospel of the Kingdom is we must obey all that Jesus commanded. It's not pray a prayer and you will go to heaven. It's accept Jesus and His finished work on the tree and live in His Kingdom in the here and now. He's the King, so just do what He says. It's not that complicated. Religion always wants to complicate things that are simple.

Adam LiVecchi ● @adamlivecchi
The gospel of the Kingdom is we must obey all that Jesus commanded.

The simplicity of the gospel is as follows. God is a Creator and man is a sinner. Jesus was fully God and fully man. He came from the womb of a virgin according to the prophecy of Isaiah. Jesus lived a sinless life. He offered His breath from the tree. He rose again on the third day. He ascended to heaven, and He is seated at God's right hand until all of His enemies become His footstool. He's coming again, and when He comes every eye will see Him. He will judge the living and the dead. He will make all things new, both heaven and earth. Those who received Him and obeyed Him will be with Him forever in paradise or heaven. Those who reject Him will burn in hell forever. Biblically speaking, the simplicity of the gospel is not up for discussion.

Living the gospel is very necessary, especially if we want to preach it and not be a hypocrite. When we preach the gospel, we must bring people to the place of decision. Even if they don't make a decision, they have just made one. The Bible says, "Today is the day of salvation." Not everyone has a tomorrow. In Haiti on January 12, 2010, because of the earthquake over 230,000 people did not have a tomorrow. I know you get the point. We must not ever forget the urgency of the gospel. The gospel is a life and death, heaven or hell issue. We don't want to be the reason someone burns in hell forever. God will not bless our silence. Jesus has entrusted the gospel to us, and we must be faithful at all costs. When people really believe in their hearts and confess with their mouths, their lives will bear witness to their words. An authentic conversion always yields a testimony. The gospel is the power of God unto salvation, and there is always manifest evidence of salvation in the life of a believer.

Questions

1. Who is the gospel for?

   _____

   _____

2. Are people who do not receive Jesus' sacrifice actually guilty of His blood?

   _____

   _____

   _____

3. If you don't preach the gospel, who will?

   _____

   _____

   _____

Prayer of Impartation

Father, I am praying that I would be so filled with the love of Jesus that I would preach the gospel fearlessly. Let Your love and burden for the lost fully overtake me. Let the passion of Jesus Christ fully consume me. Let the power of Your Kingdom be manifested as I boldly declare Christ as the only way to the Father. I pray these things in the name of Jesus Christ—the only name in which men might be saved.

GO. PREACH. HEAL.

Scriptures to Meditate On

The Spirit of the Lord God is upon me; because the Lord hath anointed me to preach good tidings unto the meek; he hath sent me to bind up the brokenhearted, to proclaim liberty to the captives, and the opening of the prison to them that are bound; to proclaim the acceptable year of the Lord, and the day of vengeance of our God; to comfort all that mourn; to appoint unto them that mourn in Zion, to give unto them beauty for ashes, the oil of joy for mourning, the garment of praise for the spirit of heaviness; that they might be called trees of righteousness, the planting of the Lord, that he might be glorified (Isaiah 61:1-3).

And it shall come to pass, that whosoever shall call on the name of the Lord shall be saved. Ye men of Israel, hear these words; Jesus of Nazareth, a man approved of God among you by miracles and wonders and signs, which God did by him in the midst of you, as ye yourselves also know: him, being delivered by the determinate counsel and foreknowledge of God, ye have taken, and by wicked hands have crucified and slain: whom God hath raised up, having loosed the pains of death: because it was not possible that he should be holden of it (Acts 2:21-24).

For the wages of sin is death; but the gift of God is eternal life through Jesus Christ our Lord (Romans 6:23).

GIVING

Often when someone becomes born again they go from greedy to generous almost overnight. It happened to me. When I was a first-class sinner, I wouldn't give you anything. When Jesus came in, immediately I became generous because He is. Our Father is the biggest giver; He loved us so much He gave us what was most valuable to Him—Jesus. There is no such thing as a stingy Christian. I would seriously question people who say they are Christian but are not generous givers. Giving is worship, and no I am not taking an offering. Not everyone is rich monetarily. Another way people give is through hospitality. I have learned this from my parents; they are some of the most giving people I have ever met. Their gift of hospitality is actually generosity manifested through them giving time, money, and service. Hospitality is not just about giving money; it is about giving yourself. It is about an invitation into an atmosphere where you are loved, valued, and accepted. There are people who talk about the Kingdom but they are not hospitable. We need to become hospitable because God is hospitable. Often people want to talk about discipling nations but don't want to feed a poor family after church on Sunday. Friends, it is time to wake up and love in deed and in truth.

On the mission field I have been to some of the poorest places on earth. I've been to garbage dumps where thousands of people live and eat. I have been in refugee camps and slums you probably wouldn't want to be anywhere near at sundown. I guess you understand that I have been to some jacked-up places. What's interesting about the people there is whatever they have they will give. The poor and the persecuted are often the most generous. They are those who will give until it hurts and then they will give themselves if necessary.

> **Adam LiVecchi** ✔ @adamlivecchi
> Our Father is the biggest giver; He loved us so much He gave us what was most valuable to Him—Jesus.

I will tell you a very moving story about my good friend Jordan Ambroise from Carrefour, Haiti. On January 12, 2010 both he and I, by the grace of God, survived the earthquake. As the tremors continued and houses around us were still collapsing in the neighborhood, he went back into the house that was split in half and more than halfway collapsed. I specifically told him don't go in there, yet he went to get my stuff anyway. He got my passport, computer, briefcase, netbook, Bible, two watches, and my wedding ring. I was really upset that he went in there and risked his life for my material possessions, but I was also very grateful to have my stuff back. Later I asked him, "Why in the world did you go back in there?"

He smiled, looked at me, and said, "You are my guest." I began to weep, and even as I am writing I am weeping. In his world, love takes risks for guests.

This had a profound impact on me and still continues to if I stop to think about it. That is true Kingdom hospitality. Meaningful giving is not just about money, but it's about giving ourselves. Kingdom people are generous and willing to give of their money, time, and possessions—even of themselves if necessary. God expects us to give others the mercy they don't deserve. He expects us to feed the multitude with our lunch. In the economy of God, there is always enough. One of the things that marks historic revivals is radical generosity. All my good friends are radical givers; I don't want to have any greedy friends. I encourage you to surround yourself with givers. Remember, love gives, so love on someone today in Jesus' name.

Questions

1. Would you buy strangers food the next time you go out to eat? (Or you can save money so that the next time you go out to eat you treat a stranger to eat.)

    _____

    _____

    _____

2. Would you find a homeless person or someone who is down and out and take them out to eat or even to your house?

    _____

    _____

    _____

3. If God asked you, would you empty your pockets or even your bank account?

    _____

    _____

    _____

Prayer of Impartation

Father, I ask You to impart to me the gift of generosity and hospitality. Let my life choices open up the doors of destiny to others as I embrace those whom others won't. Father, be glorified in my giving. Let it be done in the right spirit, and let my motives stay pure. Establish the work of my hands and let me be the lender and not the borrower. Let people encounter Jesus through this gift You have just released to me. I ask these things in Jesus' name.

Scriptures to Meditate On

Send them away, that they may go into the country round about, and into the villages, and buy themselves bread: for they have nothing to eat. He answered and said unto them, Give ye them to eat. And they say unto him, Shall we go and buy two hundred pennyworth of bread, and give them to eat? (Mark 6:36-37)

And he looked up, and saw the rich men casting their gifts into the treasury. And he saw also a certain poor widow casting in thither two mites. And he said, of a truth I say unto you, that this poor widow hath cast in more than they all: for all these have of their abundance cast in unto the offerings of God: but she of her penury hath cast in all the living that she had (Luke 21:1-4).

Charge them that are rich in this world, that they be not highminded, nor trust in uncertain riches, but in the living God, who giveth us richly all things to enjoy; that they do good, that they be rich in good works, ready to distribute, willing to communicate (1 Timothy 6:17-18).

PROPHETIC GIFTS

Word of Knowledge, Word of Wisdom, and Prophecy

Prophetic evangelism is evangelism made easy. When you have information from God about someone whom you never met before, it changes everything. Countless times I have seen the Lord open and soften the hardest hearts through a prophetic word. Many times the results of a truly prophetic word from God are healing and salvation, which in the Greek is one word—*sozo*. Jesus moved in the prophetic gifts that Paul the apostle listed in First Corinthians 12. First Corinthians 14:31 states, *"For ye may all prophesy one by one, that all may learn, and all may be comforted."* Paul wanted everyone to learn to prophesy. Learning involves making mistakes. Control freaks are afraid of mistakes; insecure people are afraid of mistakes. People with an unhealthy fear of the Lord are afraid to do anything outside of what they know for certain will work. So many people, especially leaders, are afraid to make mistakes. If you are afraid to make mistakes as a leader, you will create a sterile atmosphere. Some people are so afraid to make mistakes they don't even try. It's okay to be wrong; it's not okay to stay wrong.

In the body of Christ the prophetic has been abused, misused, and even sold. "Prophets for profit" and a lot of the prophetic movement nowadays are really a joke. For that I do apologize. Just because there is a nutri-grain prophetic movement that is nutty, fruity, and flaky doesn't mean there isn't an authentic and healthy prophetic movement that God wants to establish in His church today. Notice I said His church, not yours or mine.

Remember this, what is entrusted to you doesn't belong to you; it belongs to Jesus, so be careful how you handle it. The prophetic that Jesus operated in and that is seen in the New Testament was used to build and advance the Kingdom of God on earth. Here are a few examples: Acts 10, Acts 13:2, Acts 16:9-10. The healthiest and most true application of the prophetic is for Kingdom advancement. The Kingdom advances through the proclamation of the gospel. The prophetic declares when, where, and how. The Holy Spirit leads us prophetically. In it the church grows and is edified. However, edification is not just tickling the ears of people and telling them that they are the greatest thing since sliced bread. Most prophecy you will hear today in the church building is actually flattery with an agenda behind it. It's okay. God will deal with all that stuff, and He is dealing with it now. The greatest way for the false or tainted to be exposed is by the pure, the real, and the raw to be demonstrated in love and truth. With that being said, let's define some things.

Adam LiVecchi ✔ @adamlivecchi
Paul wanted everyone to learn to prophesy. Learning involves making mistakes.

(These are my definitions. They are not in the Bible. I will explain them briefly and give you a context to help you understand them and operate in them as the Holy Spirit leads you.)

- Word of knowledge: divine knowledge about the past or present.

- Word of wisdom: a specific word that helps someone get where God's taking them. Wisdom is a vehicle to destiny.

- Prophecy: foretelling future events. Prophecy is an invitation to what could be, not always a foretelling of what will be.

Now that these three terms have been briefly defined let us see them in action in the Bible. From there we will learn how to receive them and give them. All of this is about relationship with Jesus and not just about entertaining conference junkies.

Word of Knowledge

> He first findeth his own brother Simon, and saith unto him, We have found the Messias, which is, being interpreted, the Christ. And he brought him to Jesus. And when Jesus beheld him, he said, Thou art Simon the son of Jona: thou shalt be called Cephas, which is by interpretation, A stone (John 1:41-42).

The **word of knowledge** was "*Thou art Simon the son of Jona.*" Here Jesus knew Peter's name without being told it. On top of that, Jesus knew his father's name as well. The word of knowledge had specific details because it is in line with how the Holy Spirit speaks "expressly or distinctly."

The **prophecy** was "*thou shall be called Cephas.*" Prophecy gives identity. Jesus was telling Peter who he would become. Identity precedes assignment. Before Jesus told Peter He would make him a fisher of men, He told him he was Simon and he would be called Cephas. Jesus knew who Peter was, where he was from, and who he was becoming.

Word of Wisdom

> And when they wanted wine, the mother of Jesus
> saith unto him, They have no wine. Jesus saith unto
> her, Woman, what have I to do with thee? mine hour
> is not yet come. His mother saith unto the servants,
> Whatsoever he saith unto you, do it (John 2:3-5).

The **word of wisdom** was "*Whatsoever he saith unto you, do it.*" The Word of wisdom is also something that activates the gift of miracles. Wisdom is a vehicle that established the purposes of God.

Prophecy

> And he saith unto him, Verily, verily, I say unto you,
> Hereafter ye shall see heaven open, and the angels of
> God ascending and descending upon the Son of man
> (John 1:51).

The **prophecy** was "*Hereafter ye shall see heaven open, and the angels of God ascending and descending upon the Son of man.*" Here Jesus is prophesying about something that will be seen in relation to Him. The prophetic and the open heaven find their purpose in Christ and His body. The prophetic is to reveal Jesus and strengthen His body and advance His Kingdom. Here Jesus prophesied what would later happen in Luke 22:43.

Three Gifts Operating Together

Let's say I am walking down the street in New York City. I see a man sitting at the bus stop reading on his iPad. As I walk by, I have a thought in my mind that he is having marriage problems. I stop and go over to him and engage in a friendly conversation. It begins very casual, like, "How do you like your iPad Air 2?"

He replies, "Love it." I then ask him if he is having some marriage troubles. He proceeds to ask me, "Are you a psychic?"

I reply, "No sir."

He then asks, "How did you know that?"

I reply, "God loves you and He even likes you and cares about your life and family, and so He decided to tell me this because He wants to restore your marriage."

I then very casually mention to him an amazing book that changed my life called *Love and Respect*. He shows some interest in the book because he loves his wife and his children. I ask him if I can see his iPad Air 2; he says, "For what?"

I reply, "I am going to buy you that book and have it delivered to your house." He apprehensively says, "Okay, thanks a lot." After I buy him the book, I ask him if I can pray for him. He replies, "Sure." I pray for him and give him the card of my pastor friend who is a marriage counselor. I mention that this man will do marriage counseling if he would like, and it's free. He says, "Free?"

I reply, "Yes, buddy."

He goes, "Well, I thought all Christians were crooks like those TV preachers always asking for money."

I say, "No, there are lots of genuine Christians." I tell him God will restore his marriage! He smiles with a tear in his eye and says thank you. His bus comes and he gets on and goes to work.

The **word of knowledge** was when the thought came into my mind that he was having marriage troubles. Don't disregard the thoughts in your mind—you have the mind of Christ. Sometimes by ignoring your thoughts you are actually telling the Christ in you to be quiet because you don't believe Him.

The **word of wisdom** was when I told him about the book and mentioned to him about my pastor friend who does free marriage counseling.

The **prophecy** was when I told him that God would restore his marriage.

The word of knowledge was to get his attention. The word of wisdom was so that the prophetic word would be manifested and experienced. If that man goes and cheats on his wife with his secretary, it's not that the prophetic word was false; it's that he didn't hear and act on the wisdom that he was given. Prophecy comes in two ways. "No matter what" prophecy is like the second coming of Jesus. It's going to happen, like it or not. Then there is prophecy that could be but requires us to walk in obedience. For example, God told Moses he was going to lead the people into the Promised Land, but he didn't. God is not a liar and He didn't give a false prophecy. Moses hit the rock when God told him to speak to it. The people still drank because God is good. However, his disobedience cost him and his followers their destiny in the Promised Land. If you want to live out the prophetic word over your life, listen carefully to God and obey exactly what He commands.

This has been too brief to really fully explain the prophetic gifts. If you would like to read more, see our prophetic manual entitled *Listen. Learn. Obey.* (co-written with John Natale). It is more extensive on the prophetic and I recommend you get your hands on it. It is available on www.weseejesusminstries.com on the store page.

How to Receive from God

- Often we need to be quiet if we want to hear from God.

- Don't discredit your thoughts, because you have the mind of Christ.

- The posture of humility causes us to hear from God. Humility makes us irresistible to the Father just like Jesus was.

Adam LiVecchi ✔ @adamlivecchi
Don't discredit your thoughts, because you have the mind of Christ.

- God speaks through the Scriptures. Don't get discouraged if you are reading the Bible and feel like you are not getting a lot from it. Just keep reading; you are actually making a deposit into your spiritual account. The Holy Spirit will quicken you and will make a withdrawal, so to speak, when necessary.

- God speaks through dreams and visions so pay attention to your dreams and visions. Write them down, pray over them, and find a mature prophetic person to help you through coming into a clear understanding of what God is speaking to you.

In a dream, in a vision of the night, when deep sleep falleth upon men, in slumberings upon the bed; then he

openeth the ears of men, and sealeth their instruction
(Job 33:15-16).

God seals up counsel in your heart while you sleep. So don't discredit your dreams because God does give people direction in their dreams. Often what God speaks in the night seasons He confirms in the daytime. Joseph's dream saved the world. His dream was prophetic about the famine that was to come. Again, God can and will give you a word of knowledge, a word of wisdom, and a prophetic word through your dreams, so pay attention.

Some Rules of Engagement

I have learned through making mistakes, and so I am sharing my experiences with you. I hope my mistakes save you from unnecessary ones. If you are smart, you will learn from my mistakes.

- Don't say, "Thus saith the Lord" or "God says." If God really said it, they will know—trust me. Saying it in those words can be borderline manipulative.

- Don't prophesy with the wrong motives. That is between you and the Holy Spirit. Prophecy is not flattery in the name of Jesus for your personal gain.

- Don't be afraid to be wrong. If you make a mistake, humble yourself and ask the person to forgive you. Your humility will impress them more than your prophetic word.

- The key to a long-lasting and effective prophetic ministry is integrity.

- Prophecy is not for sale! Don't prostitute the anointing.

- Don't use the prophetic to vent on someone publicly whom you should have spoken to privately. The pulpit is not for you to vent on people.

- Ask God—is now the time for the word You gave me? The timing is huge, especially in the prophetic.

- Give the word how you receive it.

- It's okay to ask questions instead of making declarative statements. Here is a brief example. Let's say you are praying for someone and a thought flies through your mind that this person hates his or her father. You don't say, "Jesus says you hate your father." You don't add to the word and say, "Your father left you and that is why you hate him." Don't add to or take away from the word. Ask the person "Do you have any hatred toward your father?" Your question allows you to be wrong and them the opportunity to respond. If they say yes you most likely will have a successful time of ministry after that. If they say no, just humbly ask them to forgive you and continue ministering to them.

- The prophetic opens up in conversations. Jesus with the woman at the well in John 4 is a perfect example. One detailed word of knowledge led to a whole city receiving Jesus. The prophetic can open up cities and nations to the gospel. So be faithful with what God shows you and He will increase your influence.

METHODOLOGY

As I have traveled to different churches and nations I have been able to see some interesting stuff. As an itinerant minister I get to observe some things I would do if I were a pastor and some things that I would not do. What I have seen is that people do things very differently, yet often with the same goal in mind—to glorify Jesus and advance His Kingdom. As a person from New Jersey, I know that there are several ways to get from New Jersey to New York City. You can take a bridge, a tunnel, or a ferry; you can fly in via helicopter or even airplane. If New York is your destination, there are various ways to get there. We know there is only one way to God and that is through Jesus Christ.

Don't worry, I am not going to end with any heresy—just relax. What I am saying is that people have very different methods of bringing people to Jesus or bringing Jesus to people. People operate differently using the same spiritual gifts. Some think you should preach to the hungry before you feed them. Some of the people who think this have never been hungry before. Some people think you should feed the hungry first and then preach to them. That is fine, but if the preacher is no good they will fall asleep. As long as our methods don't violate the word of God, they are okay and shouldn't be a source of division. Sadly, often they are an unnecessary source of division because some people love to be in control. If you are someone who loves to be in control, you probably won't be a great team player until your control issue meets Jesus on the cross.

> ![Adam LiVecchi avatar] **Adam LiVecchi** ✔ @adamlivecchi
> Methods are okay, but don't put your trust in them.
>
> ◯ ⟲ ♡ ✉

Here is an example of two different methods of reaching people with the same goal of salvation in mind. Jude 1:22-23 states, "*And of some have compassion, making a difference: and others save with fear, pulling them out of the fire; hating even the garment spotted by the flesh.*" The methods are fear and compassion. Sometimes your compassion will cause others to come to Christ. Other times, it's fear of God or hell that will bring others into the Kingdom. For me it was the latter. I got saved because the Lord Jesus spoke to me and said, "Adam, you really, really need Me." The fear of the Lord came on me; I got on my knees and got born again in my room. God scared the hell out of me! The fear of the Lord made me run to Him, not from Him.

We shouldn't shy away from talking about hell because other people have used it the wrong way or were not being led by the Holy Spirit when they talked about it. It is the Holy Spirit who will lead you into the proper method for the moment. He is the God of all flesh, and flesh is subject to time. He knows exactly how to lead you and when, so just pay attention to his voice. Methods are okay, but don't put your trust in them. God is outside the box, but He is inside His word. His word is a light for your feet, so you are going places, and remember you are not alone. The Holy Spirit will reveal the word so you can apply the truth and minster Jesus to people. I have the utmost confidence in the Holy Spirit's ability to lead you.

Questions

1. Think of some creative ways you can bring the love, power, and truth of Jesus to those who don't know Him. Write three ways down and act on them. Remember, your actions may cause someone else to have an encounter with God.

   _____

   _____

   _____

   _____

2. Do you think healthy dialogue can put an end to a lot of unnecessary division?

   _____

   _____

   _____

   _____

3. If the truth line is crossed, should you continue to work with someone?

   _____

   _____

   _____

   _____

Prayer of Impartation

Father, in Jesus' name cause me to put my full trust in Your ability to lead me and use me to advance Your Kingdom. Let me receive creative methods that bring Jesus to people without ever compromising the truth of Your word. Bless me in every endeavor I do to advance Your Kingdom. I ask these things in Jesus' name.

IMPARTATION

Let me tell you a brief story about spiritual hunger, risk, and impartation. It was the spring of 2009. I was scheduled to go to São Paulo, Brazil to minster in a few churches with my friend Teofilo Hayashi's ministry school, "Dunamis." I was excited because it was my first time being in Brazil. When he picked me up from the airport, he welcomed me and said, "The heavenly man is in Brazil and we are going to see him tonight."

Immediately after those words came out of his mouth, I knew that this man must lay hands on me and pray for me. So we went to the church and there were over 3,000 people. The place was jam-packed. As we were walking through the crowd I sarcastically said, "Teofilo, I don't know why they didn't save us a front-row seat." As we continued to walk through the crowd, I realized that they did. Brother Yun, also known as the heavenly man, was preaching. He was preaching in Chinese and it was getting translated from Chinese to German to Portuguese, meaning I didn't have a clue what he was saying. All I knew was you could have dropped a pin in the room and you would have been able to hear it. Every eye was on this man, and as I looked around I noticed that people were listening very intently. What was interesting was that I sat there weeping but not having any clue what the heck the guy was saying. There is a great lesson in that, which is that the Holy Spirit can move on you even when you don't understand what is happening. God really is in control.

My friend Teofilo briefly summed up the sermon. He was basically saying, "You are the five loaves and two fish in the hands of Jesus.

How much can He break you and pass you out?" Ouch, not too seeker friendly, eh?

When Brother Yun had finished preaching, we made a run for the stage trying to see if he would pray for us. The hunger was not about man, but we could see Jesus in this man and we wanted him to lay hands on us and pray for us. We were two young men hungry for the real things, so to speak. Brother Yun didn't even look at us; his assistant just took him backstage. So Teofilo and I were like, "What are we going to do?" Both of us were resolute about not leaving before he prayed for us. So Teofilo said, "Quick, follow me."

We proceeded to move at a jog. *Where are we going?* I thought to myself. To make a long story short, we literally snuck backstage. One usher looked at us as if to say, "I know you don't really belong here," but thank the Lord he just kept walking. Another usher passed by, and Teofilo started to speak to him in Portuguese. In about two minutes Teofilo and I were in the room waiting to be prayed for by the heavenly man. I will never forget this part.

In the room there was a tall, skinny businessman playing with his phone while he was speaking to the heavenly man. This guy, in my opinion, was totally disrespecting Brother Yun. The New Jersey side of me wanted to slap this guy in the head—in Christian love, of course. It was then when Jesus said to me, "Adam, you are standing before Me right now. You see that man—he is completely dead." As the Lord Jesus said this to me, I just began to weep. The fear of the Lord came upon me in a very strong way.

Brother Yun put his right hand on me and began to prophesy. He said, "The spirit of prophecy is upon you. You will go to dark places. You will plant churches; you will be persecuted." I hit the floor weeping, shaking, and laughing. He then laid hands on and prophesied to Teofilo that God would use him in his generation and that he would be famous and on TV, if I recall correctly. He also wound up on the floor shaking and crying as well.

Later after we got up, we went outside and had a piece of grilled corn on the cob on the street outside the church. That day we knew God marked us forever. Brother Yun bore on his body the marks of the Lord Jesus Christ. The Chinese government broke both of his legs while he was imprisoned for the gospel. The man had a house church network of over one million people before he was fifty years old. In the Kingdom of God, he is a hero. It was the privilege of a lifetime for someone like that to lay hands on me and pray for me. I would rather be prayed for by the persecuted than the famous any day. I encourage you to get his book, which is entitled *The Heavenly Man*.

In the Kingdom, sometimes you have to press in and break through in order to receive what God has for you. I encourage you to be led by the Holy Spirit, especially when it comes to having people pray a prayer of impartation for you. Many amazing friends of God have prayed for me, and I am truly grateful for their lives. Here are just some of them: Heidi and Rolland Baker, Steve and Christina Stewart, Leif Hetland, Lesley-Anne Leighton, Bill Johnson, Randy Clark, David Greco, Dr. Sandy Kirk, and Brother Yun. These are people whom Jesus shines through, and I am grateful for the grace on their lives. My prayer is that this generation that God is raising up would take the Kingdom and the mission of Jesus to the next level, whatever that looks like. I hope by the grace of God that I have stirred your hunger for Jesus and His Kingdom a bit.

Perhaps this manual has blessed you. Maybe you even learned a few things. Now is the time to put into practice that which you have learned. After you begin to consistently do what you have learned, you are qualified and responsible to teach others what you have learned. Remember, in the Kingdom all leadership is by example. Your job, should you choose to accept it, is to teach others by your example and lifestyle. That is a really good start, but there is more. As someone who has learned, you are now called to facilitate the growth of others. People don't just learn by reading. People learn by going and doing that which they have learned. We don't really know until we can demonstrate that which we have learned. Demonstrating is the key to facilitation. Now that you can demonstrate the Kingdom of God with signs and wonders, you need to create opportunities for others to do what you have learned and teach them. It is not enough for you to just know it and do it. You must create opportunities for others to learn it and do it. The reason you must do this as a believer is simply because Jesus did.

Jesus did signs and wonders, and then He commanded His disciples to do them as well. Later, before He ascended, He commanded them to teach others to observe all the things that He commanded. To simplify, you are both called and commanded to do the stuff and teach others to do it as well. I will give you a few brief examples with Jesus and Paul that will help you walk out this next stage of the ministry Jesus has called you to. (I am assuming you have learned to live godly in Christ Jesus, and that you preach and demonstrate the Kingdom of God by healing the sick and casting out demons.)

Now is the time to impart what you have learned to others. Impartation is for mutual edification and Kingdom multiplication. Everything begins and ends with Jesus, so let's start with Him. Matthew 10:1 states:

And when he had called unto him his twelve disciples, he gave them power against unclean spirits, to cast them out, and to heal all manner of sickness and all manner of disease.

Here Jesus is giving power to His twelve disciples. The word *gave* means to bestow, and it also indicates "with the palm of the hands." Luke 9:1 states, "*Then he called his twelve disciples together, and gave them power and authority over all devils, and to cure diseases.*" Again the same word for "gave" is used in the Greek. Second Timothy 1:6-7 states:

Wherefore I put thee in remembrance that thou stir up the gift of God, which is in thee by the putting on of my hands. For God hath not given us the spirit of fear; but of power, and of love, and of a sound mind.

Here Paul is speaking to his spiritual son Timothy. Paul received the truth of impartation from the ministry of Jesus. This truth is also seen from the patriarchs, from Moses to Joshua and even from Elijah to Elisha. Timothy received an impartation through the laying on of Paul's hands.

Adam LiVecchi ✔ @adamlivecchi
It's the Holy Spirit who gives gifts according to His will, but it's through your hands that He gives them.

It's the Holy Spirit who gives gifts according to His will, but it's through your hands that He gives them. Through His sovereignty He can give gifts and He does, but in His wisdom and sovereignty He has chosen to use you. It's the same with healing—Jesus is the healer, but somewhere between your hand and a sick body the power of the Lord is present to heal. Living with clean hands is a serious issue, so live holy and don't play games with God because He is not a joke. As you lay your hands on others, the Holy Spirit will release gifts according to His will. Randy Clark said something on the subject of impartation that is absolutely wonderful: "God can give you what I do not have." What I love about this statement is that the focus is on God and not on man. God uses man because Jesus put on flesh. Christ came so we could go. We are sent in His name so He would be the focus. I bless you in Jesus' name to fulfill all that God has for you.

GO. PREACH. HEAL.

Questions

1. Will you be a part of the growth of others?

   _____

   _____

   _____

   _____

   _____

2. Does God want to use you to impart to others?

   _____

   _____

   _____

   _____

   _____

3. Are you willing for God to use you in this manner?

   _____

   _____

   _____

   _____

   _____

   _____

Prayer of Impartation

Father, in Jesus' name I am blessed to heal the sick, preach the gospel, cast out demons, and even raise the dead in Your name. I agree with Your word concerning them. Release grace on them for impartation. Let me be one who facilitates the supernatural power of Jesus Christ in the life of other believers. Holy Spirit, I ask that You would distribute gifts according to Your will through their hands.

You can also use this prayer on someone else; in fact, I encourage you to. Be careful, it just may change their life.

Prayer to Be Cleansed of Any Unclean Impartation

It is rather unfortunate that I have to even write this; for that, I apologize.

Father, in Jesus' name cleanse me from every unclean impartation. Cleanse me and purify me. In Jesus' name I break off any demonic baggage that I may have received through an unclean impartation by someone who talks about Jesus and lives like the devil. Lord, let only that which is pure and holy remain on me so that I might be Your reflection in the earth. Cleanse my heart and hands in Jesus' name.

If the Holy Spirit has you mention the name of the person or persons who gave you an unclean impartation, pray for them and ask God for greater discernment. If you are not sure if you have ever received an unclean impartation, ask the Holy Spirit to reveal it to you. Remember, greater is He who is in you than he who is in the world. Psalm 51 will be a good reference point for prayer on this matter.

Scriptures to Meditate On

> Now when the apostles which were at Jerusalem heard that Samaria had received the word of God, they sent unto them Peter and John: who, when they were come down, prayed for them, that they might receive the Holy Ghost: (for as yet he was fallen upon none of them: only they were baptized in the name of the Lord Jesus.) Then laid they their hands on them, and they received the Holy Ghost (Acts 8:14-17).

> For I long to see you, that I may impart unto you some spiritual gift, to the end ye may be established; that is, that I may be comforted together with you by the mutual faith both of you and me (Romans 1:11-12).

> Neglect not the gift that is in thee, which was given thee by prophecy, with the laying on of the hands of the presbytery. Meditate upon these things; give thyself wholly to them; that thy profiting may appear to all (1 Timothy 4:14-15).

This is only the beginning...

ABOUT ADAM LIVECCHI

Adam LiVecchi, the founder of We See Jesus Ministries, has traveled the globe extensively preaching the gospel with signs and wonders following its proclamation. Pastor Adam has also helped equip the saints to hear from God and heal the sick. Pastor Adam and his wife Sarah are the founding pastors of Rescue Church. He is also an author of a growing number of books. Their goal is simple—share the love and power of Jesus so all may taste and see that the Lord is good.

Author Contact

Ministry Number: (201) 562-6335

Website: www.WeSeeJesusMinistries.com

E-mail: info@weseejesusministries.com

Church: www.RescueChurch.tv

Blog: www.AdamLiVecchi.com

Experience a personal revival!

Spirit-empowered content from today's top Christian authors delivered directly to your inbox.

Join today!
lovetoreadclub.com

Inspiring Articles
Powerful Video Teaching
Resources for Revival

Get all of this and so much more, e-mailed to you twice weekly!

LOVE TO READ CLUB
by **D DESTINY IMAGE**